Merry Christmas
to
August.
Love,
Gram.

STARS

A GUIDE TO THE CONSTELLATIONS, SUN, MOON, PLANETS, AND OTHER FEATURES OF THE HEAVENS

a Golden Guide® from St. Martin's Press

by
HERBERT S. ZIM, Ph.D., Sc.D.
and
ROBERT H. BAKER, Ph.D., D.Sc

Revised and Updated by
MARK R. CHARTRAND, Ph.D.

Illustrated by
JAMES GORDON IRVING

D0777707

St. Martin's Press ⚏ New York

FOREWORD

The artist, James Gordon Irving, worked with skill and imagination. His wife, Grace Crowe Irving, assisted in research. David H. Heeschen of the Harvard Observatory and Ivan King of the University of Illinois Observatory helped with data and tables. Paul Lehr, of the National Oceanic and Atmospheric Administration, checked text involving meteorology. Hugh Rice of the Hayden Planetarium gave helpful advice, and our seasonal constellation charts owe much to his projections. Dorothy Bennett, for many years a member of the Hayden Planetarium's staff, contributed greatly to our editorial planning. Isaac Asimov, Joe and Simone Gosner are to be credited for intermediate revisions; Mark R. Chartrand prepared the latest revision. Twelve new illustrations by Howard Friedman have been added for this edition.

Thanks are due the Lowell, Hale (Mt. Wilson and Mt. Palomar), Lick, Yerkes, and National Optical Astronomy observatories and NASA for the use of images.

CONTENTS

This is a book for the novice, the amateur, or anyone who wants to enjoy the wonders of the heavens. It is a field guide, with information to help you understand more fully what you see. Use this book when you are watching the stars, constellations, and planets. Thumb through it at odd moments to become familiar with sights you may see; carry it along on trips or vacations.

Egyptian Pyramids

Stars and planets have attracted man's attention since earliest times. Ancient tablets and carvings show that movements of planets were understood before 3000 B.C. Legend says two Chinese astronomers who failed to predict an eclipse correctly in 2136 B.C. were put to death. The Egyptians placed their pyramids with reference to the stars. The circles of stone at Stonehenge may have been used to keep track of lunar eclipses. Astronomy is indeed the oldest science, yet its importance increases as scientists turn to the stars to study problems of physics which they cannot tackle directly in the laboratory.

As far back as history records, there were professional astronomers — long before there were professional zoologists and botanists. The Egyptians, Chinese, and Europeans had court astronomers. Their work often involved trying to predict future events, but their system, though considered unscientific today, involved observation and recording of facts about stars and planets. These early astronomers, as well as those of today, made remarkable discoveries that changed man's outlook on the world and himself.

There has always been, too, an army of amateurs studying and enjoying the stars. Some make practical use of their knowledge — sailors, pilots, surveyors — but most study the heavens out of sheer interest and curiosity.

WHY LOOK?   The stars can tell you time, direction, and position. These are about their only practical use to an amateur. More important is the satisfaction one finds in recognizing the brightest stars and planets. To see and to recognize Leo in the eastern sky is akin to seeing the first robin. And, as you learn more about the stars and the variety of other celestial objects, the more the wonder of the heavens grows.

WHERE TO LOOK   Star-gazing has no geographic limits. Some stars can even be seen from brightly lit, smoky city streets, but the less interference from lights or haze the better. An ideal location is an open field, hill, or housetop where the horizon is not obscured by trees or buildings. However, buildings or a hill may also be used to screen off interfering lights, and although you may see less of the sky this way, you will be able to see that part of it better.

WHEN TO LOOK   Only the brighter stars and planets are visible in full moonlight or soon after sunset. At these times the beginner can spot them and learn the major constellations, without being confused by myriads of fainter stars. On darker nights, without moonlight, one may observe minor constellations, fainter stars, nebulae, and planets. Stars and planets visible at any given hour depend on time of night and season of the year. As the earth rotates, new stars come into view in the eastern sky as the evening progresses. Late at night one can see stars not visible in the evening sky until several months later. The

Sundial

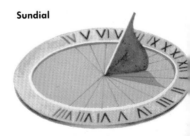

seasonal star charts (pp. 64-65, 72-73, 82-83, 90-91) and planet tables (pp. 124-125) show the location of major celestial objects at various times of the year. See check list, p. 158.

HOW TO LOOK   First, be comfortable. Looking at stars high above the horizon may cause a stiff neck and an aching back; so use a reclining chair, a couch, or a blanket spread on the ground. Remember — ground and air may be unexpectedly cold at night; warm clothing, even in summer, may be needed. How to look also involves a method of looking. The section on constellations (pages 50-101) gives suggestions. Many observations require knowing a little about angles in the sky; see p. 71. After you have become familiar with the more common stars, constellations, and planets, a systematic study may be in order — perhaps with field glasses. By that time your interest may lead you to some of the activities suggested on the following pages.

EQUIPMENT   You need no equipment, except your eyes, to see thousands of stars. This book will point the way to hours of interesting observation with your eyes alone. Later you will find your enjoyment greatly enhanced by the use of field glasses (6- to 8-power) such as those used in bird study. With these you can see vastly more — details on the moon, moons of Jupiter, many thousands of stars, star clusters, double stars, and nebulae. Larger field glasses (12-, 15-, or 18-power mounted on a tripod) will reveal finer lunar details and more hundreds of exciting stellar objects. Some day you may buy or make your own telescope.

ACTIVITIES FOR THE AMATEUR

ENJOYING THE STARS It is worth repeating that night-by-night observing, studying, and enjoying the stars is the activity that can mean the most to most people. No equipment and little preparation are needed. This book (see p. 158) and sources of information suggested (p. 11) will help.

Zeiss
Projection
Planetarium

IDENTIFICATION The enjoyment of stars involves some practice in identification. Knowing two dozen constellations and a dozen of the brightest stars is often enough. A systematic study of stars, the identification of lesser constellations, and the location and study of clusters and nebulae demand more intensive efforts. A serious amateur will benefit by knowing nearly all the constellations and bright stars before going deeper into any phase of astronomy.

FOLLOWING THE PLANETS The planets, moving along in their orbits, are constantly changing their positions. Even the beginner can become familiar with the movements of planets — can recognize them, and predict which way they will travel. Knowing the planets is as important and as enjoyable as knowing the stars.

MUSEUMS Many museums have astronomical exhibits worth seeing. These may include meteorites, photographs of stars and planets, and sometimes working models of

Hayden Planetarium

the solar system. Museums may be found at universities, observatories, planetariums, or governmental institutions. Inquire locally or when traveling concerning museums in the area that may offer astronomical exhibits.

OBSERVATORIES   These are the sites of the great optical and radio telescopes where professional astronomers work. When work is going on, astronomers cannot be disturbed. However, many observatories are open for tours at specified hours, and some offer a schedule of public lectures. Some of the major places you can visit are listed here, and others are given in references on p. 11.

> Kitt Peak National Observatory, Tucson, AZ
> National Radio Astronomy Observatory, Greenbank, WV
> Mt. Wilson Observatory, Los Angeles, CA
> U.S. Naval Observatory, Washington, DC
> Allegheny Observatory, Pittsburgh, PA

PLANETARIUMS   These "indoor universes" offer the chance to see and learn the sky under the instruction of experts. Sky shows also explain astronomical concepts. In addition to hundreds of small planetariums in schools and smaller museums, among the major planetariums are:

> Hayden Planetarium, New York, NY
> Adler Planetarium, Chicago, IL
> Fels Planetarium, Philadelphia, PA
> Griffith Planetarium, Los Angeles, CA
> Fernbank Planetarium, Atlanta, GA
> Charles Hayden Planetarium, Boston, MA
> Morrison Planetarium, San Francisco, CA
> Davis Planetarium, Baltimore, MD
> Buhl Planetarium, Pittsburgh, PA

CLUBS AND ASSOCIATIONS   Amateur astronomers often band together to share their experiences and interests. Clubs are found in most large cities and many smaller ones. At meetings, a lecture or discussion is usually followed by a period of observing through telescopes. Some clubs work on cooperative projects in which the members share some scientific investigation. Visitors are usually welcome, and membership is commonly open to anyone who is interested.

Grinding a Mirror

Through such activities anyone from a youth in high school to a retired couple can become serious amateurs. Such amateurs spend much of their time working on an astronomical hobby. They often become experts; some have made important discoveries. Professional astronomers are glad to have the help of trained amateurs, and several fields of astronomical research are manned largely by them. Amateur activities that demand greater skill and experience offer greater rewards in the satisfaction they provide.

TELESCOPE MAKING   Making a telescope requires time and patience. But in the end you have an instrument costing only a small fraction of its worth, plus the fun of having made it. The telescopes made by amateurs are usually of the reflecting type, with a concave mirror instead of a lens for gathering light. Telescope-making kits, including a roughly finished glass "blank" for the mirror, other telescope parts, and complete instructions, are available from some optical-supply firms.

Armillary Sphere Once Used to Demonstrate Celestial Motions

OBSERVING METEORS

Meteors or shooting stars (pp. 130-133) often occur in well-defined showers. Careful observation and plotting of the paths of meteors yield information of scientific value. A number of groups of amateurs are engaged in observing meteors, and any interested amateur or group of amateurs can join. Contact the American Meteor Society, Dept. of Physics and Astronomy, State University, Geneseo, NY 14454.

OBSERVING VARIABLE STARS

Amateurs with telescopes have done unusual work in this advanced field. Studies of these stars are coordinated by the American Association of Variable Star Observers, 187 Concord Ave., Cambridge, Massachusetts 02138. The director of the Association will be glad to furnish qualified amateurs with details about this work.

STELLAR PHOTOGRAPHY

Photographing the stars and other heavenly bodies is not difficult. Excellent pictures have been taken with box cameras set firmly on a table. But pictures of faint objects must be taken with a telescope or with a special camera adjusted to compensate for earth's motion. Photography is an important tool of astronomers — one which the amateur can use to good advantage.

MORE INFORMATION This book is a primer to the sky and can only introduce a story which is more fully told in many texts and popular books on astronomy.

BOOKS:

Abell, George O., *Exploration of the Universe*, 3rd ed., Holt, Rinehart, and Winston, New York, 1975. One of the best college level textbooks.

Bok, Bart J. and Priscilla E., *The Milky Way*, 4th ed., Harvard University Press, Cambridge, 1974. An engaging introduction to our own galaxy by two renowned experts.

Chartrand, Mark R., *Skyguide*, Golden Press, New York, 1982. This excellent introduction to the sky and to astronomy in general bridges the gap between books such as this one and textbooks. It contains seasonal sky maps and detailed charts of all the constellations.

Kirby-Smith, H.T., *U.S. Observatories: A Directory and Travel Guide*, Van Nostrand Reinhold, New York, 1976. Information on visiting observatories and other astronomical sites.

Lum, Peter, *The Stars in Our Heavens*, Pantheon Books, New York, 1948. A delightful recounting of sky mythology from around the world.

Mayall, Mayall, and Wyckoff, *The Sky Observer's Guide*, Golden Press, New York, 1965. An introductory book for the layman with maps of the heavens.

Norton, Arthur P., *Norton's Star Atlas*, Sky Publishing Corp., Cambridge, 1978. An excellent first sky atlas useful with binoculars or a small telescope.

Shipman, Harry L., *Black Holes, Quasars, and the Universe*, 2nd ed., Houghton Mifflin Co., Boston, 1980. An exciting introduction to recent astronomical discoveries.

MAGAZINES:

Astronomy, AstroMedia Corp., P.O. Box 92788, Milwaukee, WI 53202.

Mercury, Astronomical Society of the Pacific, 1290 24th Ave., San Francisco, CA 94122.

Sky and Telescope, Sky Publishing Corp., 49 Bay State Rd., Cambridge, MA 02138.

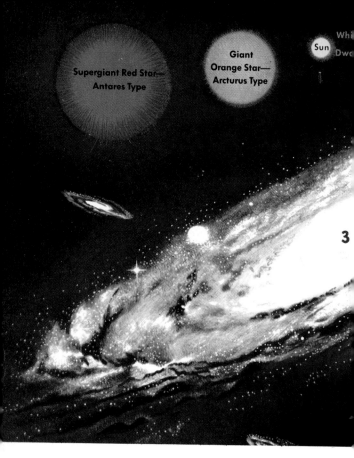

Supergiant Red Star—
Antares Type

Giant
Orange Star—
Arcturus Type

Sun

Whi
Dwa

3

OUR UNIVERSE is so vast that its limits are unknown. Through it are scattered millions of galaxies of various sizes and shapes. In a galaxy like one shown here (3), our sun and the earth are located (see p. 42). Galaxies contain hundreds of millions, even hundreds of billions, of stars of many types

(1), ranging from red supergiants less dense than the earth's atmosphere to white dwarfs hundreds of times denser than lead. Stars on the average are spaced several light-years apart, but may be closer in some clusters (2). Planets may revolve around many of the stars.

OUR SOLAR SYSTEM is located halfway from the center of our galaxy — the Milky Way. Around the sun revolve the nine major planets with more than four dozen satellites; also hundreds of thousands of asteroids and swarms of meteors. Here we see the planets (1) in their orbits around the sun (see

pp. 102-105) and (2) in the order of their size. The asteroid
Ceres is compared (3) to Texas for size, and the moon is
compared (4) to the United States. A comet's orbit (5) appears in red. Our solar system may be only one of billions in
the universe. So far, life is known to exist only on earth.

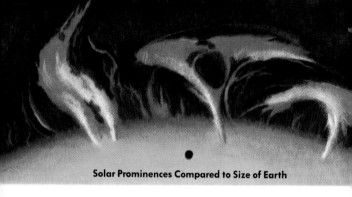
Solar Prominences Compared to Size of Earth

THE SUN is the nearest star. Compared to other stars it is of just average size; yet if it were hollow, over a million earths would easily fit inside. The sun's diameter is 860,000 miles. It rotates on its axis about once a month. The sun is gaseous; parts of the surface move at different speeds. The sun's density is a little under 1½ times that of water.

The sun is a mass of incandescent gas: its core is a gigantic nuclear furnace where hydrogen is built into helium at a temperature of millions of degrees. Four million tons of the sun's matter is changed into energy every second. This process has been going on for billions of years, and will continue for billions more.

The sun's dazzling surface, the photosphere, is speckled with bright patches and with dark sunspots (pp. 22-23). Rising through and beyond the chromosphere, great prominences or streamers of glowing gases shoot out or rain down. The corona, which is the outermost envelope of gases, forms a filmy halo around the sun.

It is unsafe to observe the sun directly with the naked eye or binoculars. Use a special filter, a dark glass, or a film negative to protect your eyes. When a telescope is used, project the sun's image on a sheet of paper.

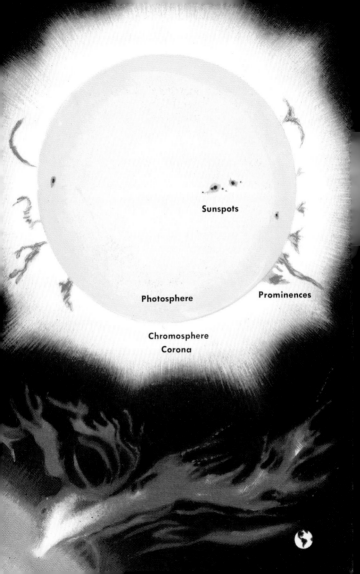

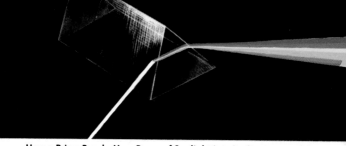

How a Prism Breaks Up a Beam of Sunlight into Its Component Colors

SUNLIGHT Every square yard of the sun's surface is constantly sending out energy equal to the power of 700 automobiles. About one two-billionth of this, in the form of sunlight, reaches us. Sunlight is a mixture of colors. When it passes through a glass prism, some of the light is bent or refracted more than other portions. Light leaving the prism spreads out into a continuous band of colors called a spectrum. Colors grade from red, which is bent least, through orange, yellow, green, and blue to violet, which is bent most.

The spectrum is crossed by thousands of sharp dark lines. These indicate that some light was absorbed as it passed through the cooler gases above the sun's surface. These gases

Fraunhofer Lines
Invisible Ultraviolet G   **F**   **E**

absorb that part of the sunlight which they would produce if they were glowing at a high enough temperature. Thus a study of the dark lines in the solar spectrum (called Fraunhofer lines, after their discoverer) gives a clue to the materials of which the sun is made. Of the 92 "natural" elements on the earth, ⅔ have been found on the sun. The rest are probably present also. From the shifting of spectral lines, astronomers can measure the rotation of the sun and the motions of stars. They can detect magnetic fields from spectral lines and can determine a star's temperature and its physical state. Although astronomers can only see the surface of a star, they can calculate what it must be like deep inside.

D   C   B   Invisible Infrared

RAINBOWS are solar spectra formed as sunlight passes through drops of water. Rainbows may be seen when a hose is adjusted to a fine spray. The drops act like prisms, refracting sunlight to produce the spectrum.

A single, or primary, rainbow has red on the outside, violet inside. The arc is 40 degrees in radius. The center of the arc is always opposite the sun. When you see a bow, the sun is behind you. Sometimes a secondary rainbow forms outside the primary. It is fainter, with colors reversed — red inside, violet outside. The secondary bow forms from light

A Rainbow Is a Spectrum

reflected twice within drops. Light may be reflected more than twice, so occasionally up to five rainbows are seen.

Another type of bow — red, or red and green — may appear with primary and secondary bows.

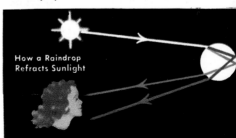

How a Raindrop Refracts Sunlight

SUNSPOTS often appear on the sun's photosphere — appearing as dark, sculptured "holes" in contrast to the bright white surface. These sunspots are sometimes so large they can be seen with the unaided eye (through a dark glass for protection, of course), and are most easily observed when the sun is low on the horizon. The use of field glasses or a small telescope helps, but the safest method of observation is to study photographs. The dark center, or umbra, of a sunspot varies from a few hundred to over 50,000 miles across. This is surrounded by a less dark area, a penumbra, that often doubles the size of the sunspot. As the sun rotates, new sunspots come into view. Most persist for a week or so, but the maximum duration is from three to four months.

The number of sunspots varies in cycles of about 11 years — first increasing steadily until hundreds of groups are seen annually, then gradually decreasing to a minimum of about 50 groups. At the beginning of a cycle the sunspots appear about 30° north and south of the sun's equator. As the cycle progresses, they develop closer to the equator and the zone of activity extends from 10 to 20

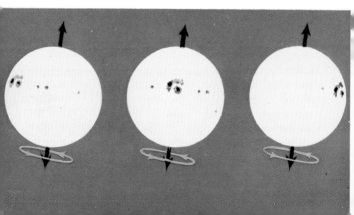

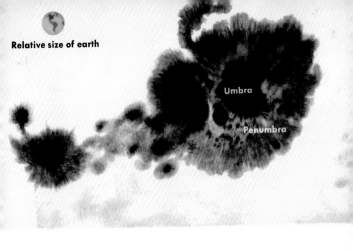

Relative size of earth

Umbra

Penumbra

degrees on either side of it. The 11-year cycle is really an average value. Mysteriously waxing and waning, the exact length of the cycle can be as short as nine years or as long as sixteen. The 11-year cycle is part of a larger 22-year cycle in which the entire magnetic field of the sun may reverse itself.

Sunspots seem to be giant magnetic storms on the sun's surface, which may be caused by deeper, periodic changes. They occur in groups which grow rapidly and then slowly decline. The gases in the sunspot (about 8,000°F) are cooler than the rest of the sun's surface (about 11,000°F); hence they appear darker. Actually, if a large sunspot could be isolated in another part of the sky, it would appear as bright as a hundred full moons. Sunspots have strong magnetic fields. Radiation from "solar flares" near them interacts with the upper levels of the earth's atmosphere and interrupts shortwave radio transmission; it is also likely to cause an increase in auroras (pp. 24-25).

AURORAS OR NORTHERN LIGHTS   The shifting, glowing, diffuse light of an aurora is hard to describe. Yellow, pink, and green lights come and go; arcs of light start at the horizon and spread upward; streamers and rays extend toward the zenith. Auroras last for hours, and often all through the night. They are most often seen in the north and middle northern latitudes and in the arctic. A similar display is seen in the southern latitudes. Auroras occur from about 60 to 600 miles up in the air. At these heights, so little air remains that space is almost empty like a

vacuum, or the inside of a neon light. The shifting glow of the aurora is essentially electrical and somewhat similar to the light from the neon signs along Main Street.

Atomic particles from the sun hitting the thin gases of the upper atmosphere is what causes auroras. The charged particles come from solar flares near sunspots. The fact that auroras are most frequent near the earth's magnetic poles emphasizes their electrical character. A few days after a large new sunspot group develops, an auroral display is likely to occur.

THE SKY FROM SUNRISE TO SUNSET   As the sun's rays pass through the earth's atmosphere, some are scattered, and a play of colors results. Blue rays are scattered most, and therefore a clear sky is typically blue. But just after sunrise and just before sunset the sun is reddish. At these times the sharply slanting sun's rays must travel a longer path through the atmosphere, and more of the blue and yellow rays are scattered out of the rays reaching your eye. The red rays, which are scattered least, come through in the largest numbers, giving the sun its reddish hue. If there are clouds and dust in the air, many of the red rays

Sunlight Passes Through a Thicker Layer of Air at Sunrise and Sunset

which filter down into the lower atmosphere are reflected, and large areas of the sky may be reddened.

Because of the bending or refraction of light, which is greater when the sun is near the horizon, you can actually see the sun for a few minutes before it rises and after it sets. Daylight is a bit longer for this reason. The closer to the horizon, the greater the refraction at sunrise or sunset. Hence, as refraction elevates the sun's disc, the lower edge is raised more than the upper. This distorts the sun, just as it is rising or setting, giving it an oval or melon-shaped appearance.

Twilight is sunlight diffused by the air onto a region of the earth's surface where the sun has already set or has not risen. Astronomical twilight is defined as the period between sunset or sunrise and the time when the sun is 18 degrees below the horizon — that is, a little over an hour.

THE TELESCOPE was first put to practical use by Galileo in 1609. Since then, it has extended man's horizons farther and has challenged his thinking more than any other scientific device. The telescope used by Galileo, the best-known kind, is the refracting telescope, consisting of a series of lenses in a tube. In a simple refractor, two lenses are used, but commonly others are added to correct for the bending of light that produces a colored halo around the image. The largest refracting telescopes are one with a 40-inch lens at the Yerkes Observatory in Wisconsin, and a 36-inch one at Lick Observatory in California.

The simple reflecting telescope has a curved mirror at the bottom of the tube. This reflects the light in converging rays to a prism or diagonally placed mirror, which sends the light to the eyepiece or to a camera mounted at the side of the tube. Since mirrors can be made larger than lenses, the largest astronomical telescopes are reflectors (see p. 30). Reflectors with mirrors

40-Inch Refractor, Yerkes Observatory

Refracting Principle

200-Inch Reflector, Palomar Mountain, Calif.

Mirror

**Reflecting
Principle**

up to 8 inches in diameter are made by amateurs as the best simple, low-cost telescope. Many astronomical bodies emit invisible radio, infrared, ultraviolet, X-ray, and gamma radiation, as well as visible light; each kind of radiation gives important information to astronomers about the physical state of the source. New types of telescopes, some of them in orbit around the earth, are used to observe these parts of the spectrum.

29

THE LARGEST TELESCOPE of the reflector type in the United States is on Palomar Mountain, near San Diego, Calif. Its 200-inch (16.6-foot) mirror is a marvel of scientific and engineering skill. The great disc of pyrex glass was cast with supporting ribs to bear its weight. It is 27 inches thick and weighs 14½ tons. Yet because of its design, every part is within two inches of the air — permitting the mirror to expand and contract uniformly with changes in temperature. The great piece of glass has been polished to within a few millionths of an inch of its calculated curve. Despite its great weight it can be tilted and turned precisely without sagging as much as the thickness of a hair. The mirror gathers about 640,000 times as much light as the human eye. With it, astronomers photograph stars six million times fainter than the faintest stars you can see, and galaxies over two billion light-years away.

Stars are suns: heavenly bodies shining by their own light and generally so far away from us that, though moving rapidly, they seem fixed in their positions. All are composed of at least 99 percent hydrogen and helium.

NUMBERS OF STARS   On the clearest night you are not likely to see more than 2,000 stars. With changing seasons, new stars appear, bringing the total visible during the year to about 6,000. A telescope reveals multitudes more. The total in our galaxy runs into billions, but even so, space is almost empty. Were the sun the size of the dot over an "i," the nearest star would be a dot 10 miles away, and other stars would be microscopic to dime-size dots hundreds and thousands of miles distant.

DISTANCES OF STARS   The nearest star, our sun, is a mere 93 million miles away. The next nearest star is 26 million million miles — nearly 300,000 times farther than the sun. For these great distances, miles are not a good measure. Instead, the light-year is often used. This is the distance that light travels in one year, moving at 186,000 miles per second: nearly 6 million million miles. On this scale the nearest star (excluding the sun) is 4.3 light-years away. Sirius, the brightest star, is 8.8 light-years off. Other stars are hundreds, thousands, and even millions of light-years away.

31

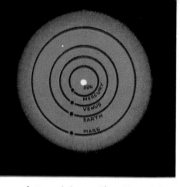

Antares Is Larger Than Mars' Orbit

STARLIGHT All stars shine by their own light. This light is produced by nuclear reactions similar to those of the hydrogen bomb occurring at the centers of stars. When the element hydrogen is transformed into helium, which happens in most stars, about 1 percent of its mass (weight) is changed into energy. This energy keeps the temperature in the star's interior at millions of degrees. At the surface the temperature varies from about 5,500 degrees F. to over 55,000 degrees, depending on the kind of star. One pound of hydrogen changing to helium liberates energy equal to about 10,000 tons of coal. In a single star the energy released in this way requires the transformation of millions of tons of matter per second.

STAR BRIGHTNESS The sun is about average in size and brightness. Some stars are up to 600,000 times as bright as the sun; others are only 1/550,000; most are between 10,000 and 1/10,000 times as bright as the sun. The brightness of a star you see depends on its distance and on its real or absolute brightness. See pp. 34-35.

STAR SIZE Most stars are so distant that their size can only be measured indirectly. Supergiant red stars are the largest. Antares has a diameter 390 times that of the sun, others are even larger. Among the small stars are white dwarfs, no larger than planets. The smallest are neutron stars that may be no more than ten miles across.

DENSITY OF STARS   The densities or relative weights of stars vary considerably. Actually all stars are masses of gas — but gas under very different conditions from those we usually see. Supergiant stars such as Antares have a density as low as 1/2,000 of the density of air. The more usual stars have a density fairly close to that of the sun. White dwarfs are so dense that a pint of their material would weigh 15 tons or more on earth. The companion to Sirius is 25,000 times more dense than the sun. Neutron stars are billions of times denser.

MOTIONS OF STARS   Our sun is moving about 12 miles per second toward the constellation Hercules. Other stars are moving too, at speeds up to 30 miles per second or faster. Arcturus travels at 84 miles per second. Many stars are moving as parts of systems or clusters. The sun and our neighborhood of the Milky Way galaxy are moving around the center of the galaxy at 150 miles per second. Some stars consist of two or more components (see p. 38) which revolve around a common center as they move together through space. The stars in a constellation do not necessarily belong together; they may be of widely differing distances from the earth and may be moving in different directions at different speeds.

COLOR OF STARS varies from brilliant blue-white to dull reddish, indicating star temperature (pp. 36-37). Only the brightest stars in the sky show colors because the eye is not sensitive to color at low light levels.

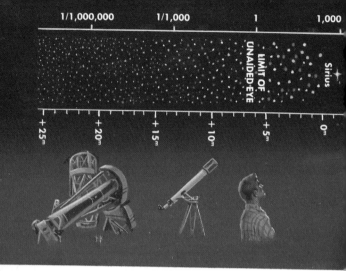

The Range of Brightnesses of Astronomical Objects

STAR MAGNITUDES   Brightness of stars is measured in terms of "magnitude." A 2nd-magnitude star is 2.5 times as bright as a 3rd, and so on throughout the scale, so that a 1st-magnitude star is 100 times as bright as a 6th. Stars brighter than 1st magnitude have zero or minus magnitude. On this scale the magnitude of the planet Venus is −4; it is 10,000 times as bright as a 6th-magnitude star, which is the faintest that the unaided eye can see. The sun's magnitude is −27.

The brightness of a star as we see it depends on two factors: its actual, or absolute, brightness and its distance from us. If one factor is known, the other can be computed. This relationship makes it possible to measure the distances of remote galaxies (p. 39).

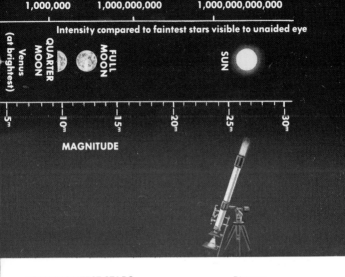

1,000,000   1,000,000,000   1,000,000,000,000

Intensity compared to faintest stars visible to unaided eye

QUARTER MOON   FULL MOON   SUN

Venus (at brightest)

MAGNITUDE

−5ᵐ   −10ᵐ   −15ᵐ   −20ᵐ   −25ᵐ   −30ᵐ

THE BRIGHTEST STARS

Name	Constellation	Magnitude as seen	Distance (light-years)	Absolute magnitude
Sirius	Canis Major	−1.5 d	9	+1.4
*Canopus	Carina	−0.7	540	−4.7
*Alpha Centauri	Centaur	−0.1 d	4	+4.3
Arcturus	Boötes	0.0	36	−0.2
Vega	Lyra	0.0	26	+0.5
Capella	Auriga	0.1	46	−0.6
Rigel	Orion	0.1 d	815	−7.0
Procyon	Canis Minor	0.4 d	11	+2.2
*Achernar	River Eridanus	0.5	127	−5.0
*Beta Centauri	Centaur	0.6	114	−2.5
Betelgeuse	Orion	0.8	652	−6
Altair	Aquila	0.8	16	+2.3
*Alpha Crucis	Southern Cross	0.9 d	260	−3.5
Aldebaran	Taurus	0.9 d	68	−0.7
Spica	Virgo	1.0	260	−3.4
Antares	Scorpius	1.0 d	425	−4.7
Pollux	Gemini	1.2	36	+1.0
Fomalhaut	Southern Fish	1.2	23	+1.9
Deneb	Cygnus	1.3	1,600	−7.3
Regulus	Leo	1.4 d	85	−0.6
*Beta Crucis	Southern Cross	1.3	490	−4.7

*Not visible at 40° N. latitude. d Double stars: combined magnitude given.

35

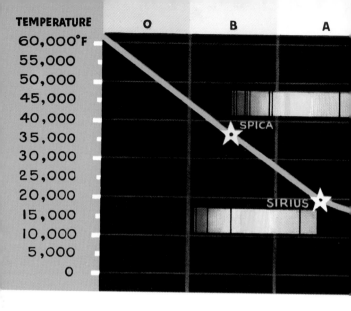

TEMPERATURE	O	B	A
60,000°F			
55,000			
50,000			
45,000			
40,000		SPICA	
35,000			
30,000			
25,000			
20,000		SIRIUS	
15,000			
10,000			
5,000			
0			

CLASSIFICATION OF STARS Over 99 percent of all the stars are classified into one of seven spectral types, depending on the appearance of the star's spectrum. The types in order of decreasing temperature are O, B, A, F, G, K, and M. Each spectral class is subdivided into 10 parts, such as A0, A1, A2, etc. To remember the types in order, say "O, Be A Fine Girl Kiss Me." The spectral appearance depends mainly on the temperature of the star's atmosphere. Different elements appear in the spectrum at different temperatures, as seen in the table opposite. A few stars of unusual types are classified as W, R, N, S, or C. In addition to spectral type, all stars may be grouped into one of the "luminosity classes": supergiants, giants, sub-giants, dwarfs (also called main sequence stars, see p. 49), and white dwarfs.

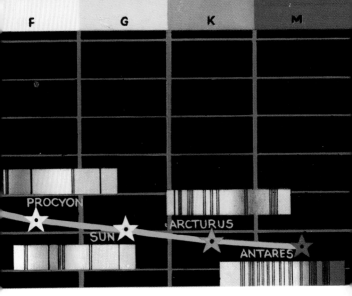

STAR CLASSIFICATION

Star class	Approx. temp. (degrees F.)	Color	Spectral character	Examples
O	over 55,000	Blue-white	Gases strongly ionized	Iota Orionis (in sword)
B	36,000	Blue-white	Strong neutral helium	Rigel Spica
A	20,000	White	Hydrogen predominant	Sirius Vega
F	13,500	Yellowish white	Hydrogen decreasing; metals increasing	Canopus Procyon
G	11,000	Yellow	Metals prominent	Sun Capella
K	7,500	Orange	Metals surpass hydrogen	Arcturus Aldebaran
M	5,500	Red	Titanium oxide present — violet light weak	Betelgeuse Antares

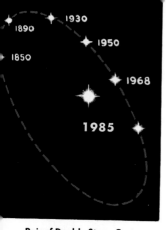

Pair of Double Stars: Castor

DOUBLE STARS About two-thirds of all known stars are double, or "binary." The components of a few can be seen with the unaided eye; thousands can be "separated" with a telescope; thousands more are detected by the spectroscope. Some stars have three or more components; Castor has six — three doubles. The main, mutually revolving pair was closest together in 1968 — about 55 times the distance of the earth from the sun.

Mizar, at the curve of the Big Dipper's handle, has a faint companion. Mizar itself is a telescopic double and the brightest component is a spectroscopic double star. When the two stars are in line, the spectra coincide. When, as they revolve, one approaches us as the other moves away, the spectrum lines are doubled. Capella and Spica are also spectroscopic double stars.

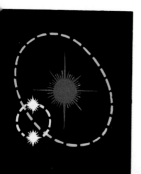

As double stars revolve, one may eclipse the other, causing reduced brightness. Best-known of eclipsing double stars is Algol, in Perseus. It waxes and wanes at intervals of about three days. The eclipsing stars are 13 million miles apart. Their combined magnitude varies from 2.3 to 3.4.

Triple Star System

VARIABLE STARS are those that fluctuate in brightness. Most dramatic are the exploding stars, the novae and supernovae. These stars rapidly grow in brilliance, up to 100,000 times or more in only a day, then fade away over months or years. Other variables change less than a magnitude. Some variables change

Nova of 1572 in Cassiopeia

regularly while others vary irregularly. Some red giants and supergiants vary from 4 to 10 magnitudes over a few months to two years. Mira, in Cetus the Whale, is a famous long-period variable that shows extreme changes of brightness.

The variables known as classical Cepheids vary in brightness over periods of one day to several weeks. The distance of any of these Cepheids can be readily estimated because of the definite relationship between its variation period and its absolute magnitude. By measuring the period, the absolute magnitude can be determined, and by comparing the absolute magnitude with the apparent magnitude, the distance can be estimated. These Cepheids are important in the calculation of distances of star clusters and galaxies (pp. 40-43).

Eclipsing Binary, Algol, with Magnitude Changes

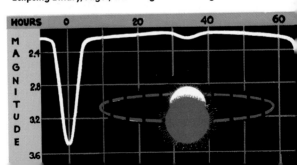

The Globular Cluster M13 in Hercules Palomar

GLOBULAR CLUSTERS are large spherical groups of old stars lying on the outskirts of our galaxy. Although they appear compact, they may be over 100 light-years across, and can contain over 100,000 stars. Somewhat over 100 have been found around our galaxy, and many more around other galaxies. Most are very distant from earth. The brightest and most famous cluster M13 shown above is 34,000 light-years away. It is barely visible to the unaided eye in the constellation Hercules; it is a small, fuzzy ball in a small telescope, but is a striking object in a large telescope.

The "Jewel Box" Open Cluster   NOAO

OPEN CLUSTERS are smaller, less populous and less regular groups of stars lying near and in the spiral arms of the galaxy. Over 300 such clusters are known, containing from a few dozen to several hundred stars. Among the more famous are the Pleiades and Hyades, in the constellation Taurus, and Praesepe (The Beehive) in Cancer. Stars in open clusters (also sometimes called galactic clusters) are much less close together than the stars in globular clusters, and are usually younger and richer in elements heavier than hydrogen and helium, having been enriched by debris from older stars.

41

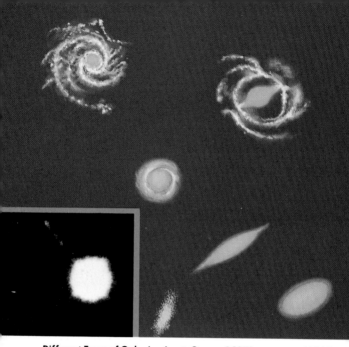

Different Types of Galaxies. Inset: Quasar 3C273 NOAO

GALAXIES are the largest forms in the universe, "islands" of a few million to hundreds of billions of stars, nebulae, gas, and dust. Some, like our Milky Way and the nearby Andromeda galaxy (M31), are spiral-shaped, over 100,000 light-years across but only a few thousand light-years thick. Other spirals have a bar across them. Still other galaxies are spheroidal or ellipsoidal in shape; some are irregular. All galaxies rotate about their centers. Stars at different distances from the galactic center move at

The Great Spiral Galaxy M31 in Andromeda   Mt. Wilson

different speeds. Extremely luminous, very distant objects called quasars are probably very young galaxies. As we look out to the depths of the universe we are seeing back in time, for it takes light time to get here across the billions of light-years. Some unusual galaxies are strong sources of radio waves. Some seem to throw off jets of high-speed, very hot gas. Many galaxies occur in clusters. Only a few nearby galaxies are bright enough to be seen in small telescopes.

Photo of Dense Section in Milky Way Yerkes

THE MILKY WAY forms a huge, irregular circle of stars tilted about 60 degrees to the celestial equator. Even before the structure of our galaxy was known, the great astronomer Herschel proposed that this concentration of stars was due to the galaxy extending farther in space in some directions than in others. It is now clear that in looking at the Milky Way you are looking down the long direction of our galaxy. As you look through a deeper layer of stars, the stars appear more numerous. The Milky Way has both thin and congested spots. In Sagittarius it is at its brightest, but all of it is a wonder to behold.

LOOKING OUT OF GALAXY

LOOKING INTO
OUTER EDGE
OF GALAXY

SUN AND EARTH

LOOKING
INTO GALAXY
TOWARDS CONGESTED CENTER

HALF OF GALAXY IN SECTION

NEBULAE is a term (Latin for "clouds") applied to distant hazy spots in the sky revealed by telescopes. They are clouds of microscopic dust and hydrogen gas within our galaxy. Of the closer nebulae, the brightest is the Great Nebula in the sword of Orion — diameter 26 light-years, distance 1,625 light-years. The entire region of Orion has the faint glow of nebulae, but here the glow is strongest. All such nebulae are faint; only long-exposure photographs bring out details of most.

"Horse-head"   Mt. Wilson

Luminous nebulae are found close to bright stars. Shortwave light from these stars stimulates the nebulae to glow like fluorescent lamps. The brightest nebulae are associated with the hottest stars. Low-temperature stars do not cause nebulae to fluoresce, but starlight scattered by the nebulae provides some illumination.

"Coal Sack" in Crux   Mt. Wilson

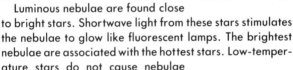

Some nebulae, having no stars nearby, are dark. They may obscure bright parts of the Milky Way and be visible as silhouettes. A series of such dark nebulae divides the Milky Way from Cygnus to Scorpius into two parallel bands. Most spectacular of dark nebulae is the "Horse-head Nebula" in Orion. Another is the "North American Nebula" in Cygnus near the star Deneb.

Trifid Nebula in Sagittarius Mt. Wilson

PLANETARY NEBULAE appear roughly spherical in shape. They have nothing to do with planets, but are actually

Owl Nebula in Ursa Major
Mt. Palomar

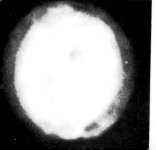

enormous globes of gas surrounding some very hot stars. Many of them look like smoke rings because we see right through their thin centers. Most are very faint, but such famous ones as the Ring Nebula in Lyra and the Owl Nebula in Ursa Major appear spectacular in long-exposure photographs.

Gaseous Nebula in Orion　　　　　　Mt. Wilson

Dust and gas, in the spiral arms of our galaxy, make it hard to determine colors, brightness, and distances of many stars. Dust makes stars behind it look redder, or may obscure them entirely. Bright gas clouds have helped astronomers to trace the spiral arms of our galaxy. Increasingly effective in this work has been the use of radio telescopes, which receive radio signals that help to identify many chemical compounds in the clouds.

Ring Nebula in Lyra　　Lick

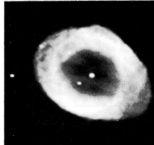

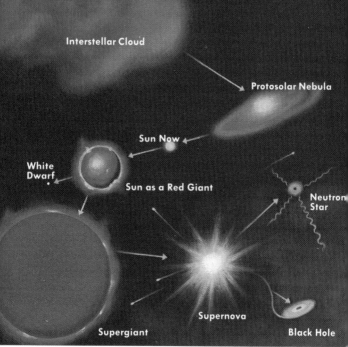

Steps in the Evolution of Stars

THE ORIGIN OF STARS lies in clouds of interstellar gas and dust. Gravity pulls the atoms together into a protostellar nebula, which contracts and heats up and begins to glow. As the cloud shrinks, the center reaches millions of degrees, hot enough for the nuclear fusion which makes a star's energy. Much of the surrounding gases are then blown away and the star settles down to the main part of its life. How large it is, how long it will live, and what its temperature (hence color) and brightness are depend on the mass (amount of material) of the star.

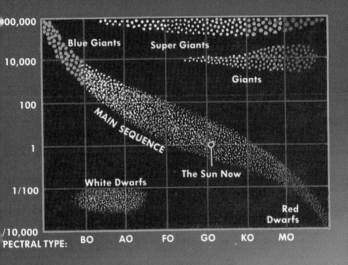

Graph of the Sun's Properties as It Evolves

More massive stars are larger and hotter, and live shorter lives. After millions to trillions of years, the star runs out of hydrogen fuel in its center, and swells and cools to become a red giant. Sometimes more massive stars swell even more to become supergiants. Almost all stars eventually contract to become white dwarfs; a few explode as supernovas, leaving behind quickly rotating neutron stars called pulsars. Astronomers use diagrams like the one above to trace the lives of stars. More than 95 percent of all stars lie in the central band called the main sequence.

Stars can be weighed and measured, and their brightness, color, and motions have meaning. Constellations are different. They are but figments of man's imagination — handy inventions to help map the sky. Some of these apparent patterns were known and used by our forefathers for thousands of years. Other minor constellations were invented by 17th-century astronomers. People in different parts of the world imagine the stars represent different shapes and things. Most of the characters and objects of the constellations we use come from the myths of the Greeks and Romans.

Although they seem unchanged for a lifetime, even a century, the constellations are changing; the stars in them are gradually shifting their positions. In any constellation some stars may be farther away than others and unrelated to them. They may differ in direction of movement as well as color or spectral class. Because of precession (p. 53), different stars have been and will become the North Star. Many constellations have been recognized since ancient times. Their boundaries were irregular and often vague until astronomers finally established them definitely by international agreement.

Amateurs nevertheless learn stars most easily by using constellations. Use the charts in this section. Constellations near the North Pole are charted on pp. 54-55, and south circumpolar constellations on pp. 98-99. For middle-latitude constellations, you will find a map for each of the four seasons, showing major constellations visible during that season in the north temperate zone.

The dome of the heavens is hard to represent on a flat map. The seasonal maps are designed to show most accurately constellations in middle north latitudes. Distortion

Big Dipper in 20th Century, with Stars Moving in Direction of Arrows

is greatest near the horizons and in the south. Constellation shapes are truer in the 28 individual constellation pictures in this section. Here they are upright. (For their positions relative to each other, see the seasonal maps.) Polaris is always at about the north celestial pole; where it is not shown, an arrow frequently points toward it.

For a complete list of constellations, see pp. 156-157.

Bright stars have names, often Arabic, and are labeled usually in order of brightness by Greek letters and constellation name, as Alpha Scorpii, brightest star in Scorpius, and Beta Cygni, second brightest in Cygnus. Symbols are used in charts in this book as follows:

★   Stars: 1st magnitude   (brighter than 1.5)
◆   2d magnitude   (1.5 to 2.5)
●   3d magnitude   (2.6 to 3.5)
·   4th and 5th magnitude (fainter than 3.5)
∴   Star clusters and nebulae

Big Dipper in A.D. 100,000

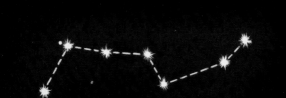

CIRCUMPOLAR CONSTELLATIONS

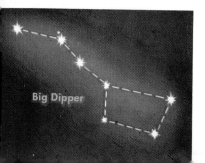

Little Dipper

The term circumpolar constellations implies that the observer is somewhere between the equator and the pole. Each 24 hours, as the earth turns on its axis, the sky seems to wheel overhead. To an observer in the north temperate zone, stars near the North Pole remain in view as they swing around; stars near the equator rise and set.

At the pole, all constellations are circumpolar; at the equator, none. For places between, the latitude is important, for if a star or constellation is nearer to the pole than the pole is to the horizon, it becomes circumpolar and does not set. The bowl of the Big Dipper does not set at latitude 40 degrees north, but in Florida, at latitude 30 degrees, it does set and so is no longer circumpolar. When the sun is north of the equator during the summer, it becomes a circumpolar star north of the Arctic Circle. The circumpolar constellations are easy to learn, and you will find them the best place in which to begin your identification of the stars. Once you know the Big Dipper, the rest fall into line.

The Little Dipper, Cassiopeia, Cepheus, Draco, and Perseus will guide you to the other constellations shown on the seasonal charts later in this book.

Big Dipper

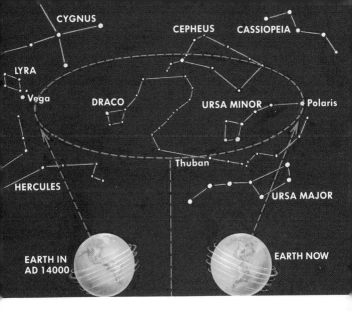

PRECESSION is the term given to a slow wobbling motion of the earth caused by the pull of the moon and sun. It is rather like the wobbling of a spinning top. Just as the axis of the top moves around in a circle, so too the earth's axis — the North and South Poles — moves around a circle and points to different locations in the sky. This means that the North Star, the star closest to being directly over earth's North Pole, changes with time. One wobble takes about 26,000 years. Today Polaris is the North Star, less than 1 degree from the true pole; at the time of the Egyptians, it was Thuban in Draco; in A.D. 14,000, Vega in Lyra will be the closest bright star to the pole, though it will be more than 5 degrees away. Precession changes which constellations are visible from a given location and at what season.

53

NORTH CIRCUMPOLAR CONSTELLATIONS

At about 40 degrees north latitude the following are considered the major circumpolar constellations: Big Dipper (Ursa Major); Little Dipper (Ursa Minor); Cassiopeia, the Queen; Cepheus, the King; Draco, the Dragon. To locate these constellations, use the accompanying chart. Facing north, hold the opened book in front of you so that the current month is toward the top. The constellations are now about as you will see them during the current month at 9 p.m. To see how they will appear earlier, turn the chart clockwise; for a later time, counterclockwise. A quarter of a turn will show how much the positions of the stars will change during a six-hour period.

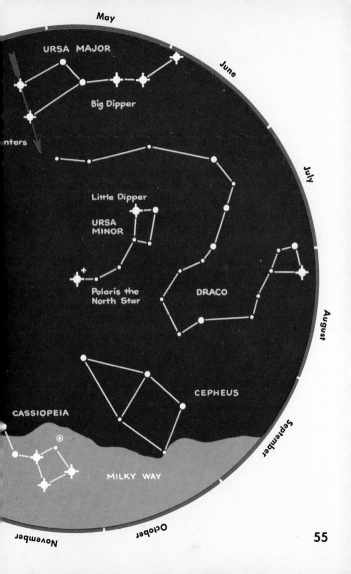

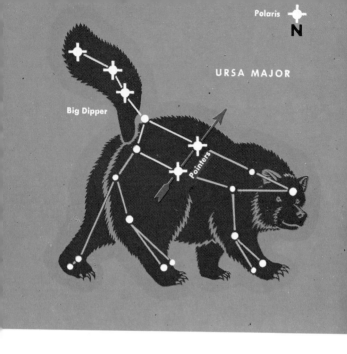

URSA MAJOR, THE GREAT BEAR (BIG DIPPER) The familiar Big Dipper is only part of the Great Bear. The Dipper's seven stars are easy to find if you face north on any clear night. The two outer stars of the bowl point to the North Star, Polaris, which is about 30 degrees away. The distance between the pointers is 5 degrees. Both measurements are useful in finding your way around the sky. The middle star of the handle (Mizar) is a double star. Its 4th-magnitude companion is faintly visible, if you look carefully. The rest of the Great Bear spreads as a curve ahead of the pointers and in another curve below the bowl.

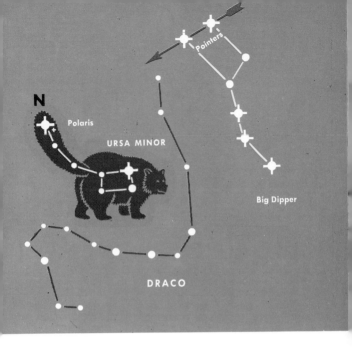

URSA MINOR, THE LITTLE BEAR (LITTLE DIPPER)

Polaris, the Pole Star, is the tail star of the Little Dipper — a dipper which has a reversed curve to the handle. Polaris is a supergiant Cepheid variable star which changes in magnitude very slightly every four days. Its distance is about 782 light-years. Polaris is not exactly at the pole but is less than a degree away; no other 2nd-magnitude star is near it. It is commonly used by navigators to determine latitude. The four stars in the bowl of the Little Dipper are of 2nd, 3rd, 4th, and 5th magnitude, making a good scale for judging the brightness of nearby stars.

57

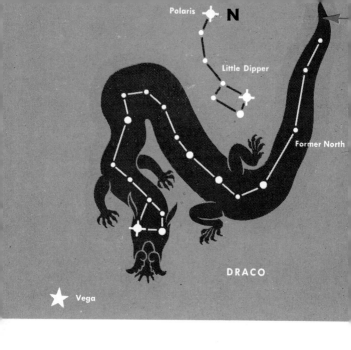

DRACO, THE DRAGON begins, tail first, about 10 degrees from the Big Dipper's pointers, and curves between the two dippers. Then it swings around the Little Dipper, doubles back, and ends in a group of four stars, forming the Dragon's head. These are about 15 degrees from Vega in Lyra. Thuban, in Draco, once the North Star, was the star by which the Egyptians oriented their famous pyramids. Though Draco is circumpolar, its faint stars are best seen in late spring and early summer, when they are highest above the northern horizon. A planetary nebula in Draco can be seen with a small telescope.

58

Nova 1572

Double Cluster

CASSIOPEIA

To Polaris

CASSIOPEIA and nearby Cepheus are involved in the myth of Perseus and Andromeda (pp. 80-81). Start at the Big Dipper, at the star where the handle and bowl meet, and sight a line through the Pole Star on to Cassiopeia. Cassiopeia has the shape of either a W, an M, or a chair, depending on how you look at it. Near the spot marked on the map appeared the famous supernova of 1572. When this explosive star appeared, it rapidly increased in magnitude until it was as bright as Venus and could be seen in daylight. Within two years it faded from view, proving that the heavens are not immutable.

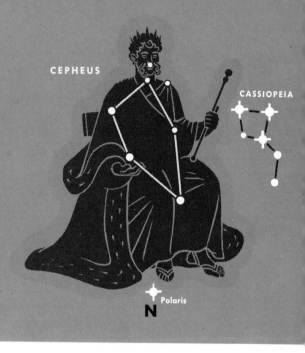

CEPHEUS

CASSIOPEIA

N Polaris

CEPHEUS is closer to the North Pole than Cassiopeia. The star shown near Cepheus' knee is about 12 degrees from Polaris on a line with the star forming the end of the W of Cassiopeia. Cepheus is a five-sided figure, like a crude, peaked house. Because of precession, the stars on the west side of Cepheus will successively become the North Star during the next 2,500 to 5,500 years. Just south of the base of Cepheus is a garnet-colored star worth spotting with binoculars. Cepheid variable stars, used in measuring distances of galaxies, are named from Delta Cephei in this constellation (see p. 39).

Circumpolar Stars as a Guide to Key Constellations

A KEY TO CONSTELLATIONS   Use the stars of the Big Dipper and other circumpolar stars to locate one or two important constellations for each season. Follow the curve of the Dipper's handle to "arc to Arcturus," or a line through the bottom stars of the Dipper to Gemini. Trace from the end of the handle through the bottom of the bowl to Leo. With these key constellations in mind, you can locate the others more easily. Be sure the constellation you are trying to locate is above the horizon at the season and hour you are looking.

CONSTELLATIONS OF SPRING

The stars of spring, summer, fall, and winter were selected as those easiest to observe at about 9:00 p.m. on the first of April, July, October, and January. The seasons actually begin a week or so earlier.

Each night at the same hour, a star appears slightly to the west of its former position. Hence stars seen in the east at 9:00 p.m. appear higher and higher in the sky at that hour as the season advances. Before April 1, spring constellations are farther to the east, and farther west after that date.

Latitude, as well as season and time of night, determines star positions. The Pole Star's height above the horizon, for example, is the same as your latitude. The seasonal maps are for about 40 degrees north latitude.

In early spring, eleven 1st-magnitude stars are in the sky at once. No other season offers so many. In addition to the constellations on pp. 66-69, look for a number of smaller ones. Between Gemini and Leo lies Cancer, the Crab, a constellation of 4th- and 5th-magnitude stars. At the center of Cancer, note the fuzzy spot. Field glasses or a small telescope brings out details of this open cluster of some 300 stars; it is Praesepe, one of the nearby clusters

in our galaxy. Another larger cluster forms Coma Berenices, Berenice's Hair. This is on a line between the tail star of Leo and the end of the Big Dipper's handle. Use field glasses.

In the southern sky are the fainter Corvus, the Crow; Crater, the Cup; and Hydra, the Water Serpent. Hydra sprawls below Leo and Virgo, the Virgin. It has one 2nd-magnitude star, the reddish Alphard. Corvus, a lopsided square of 3rd-magnitude stars, is close to Spica in Virgo (see p. 73). Crater is nearby, south of Leo. It has one 3rd-magnitude star. South of Corvus is the Southern Cross.

CONSTELLATIONS OF SPRING

About 9 p.m. in middle north latitudes

HORIZON

HERCULES

SERPENS

CORONA BOREALIS

DRACO

M13

Arcturus
BOOTES

CANES VENATICI

URSA MAJOR

Mizar

EASTERN

HORIZON

Spica

VIRGO

COMA BERENICES

LE

MINO

HYDRA

CORVUS

CRATER

LEO

Reg

SEXTAN

HYDRA

ANTLIA

SOUTHERN

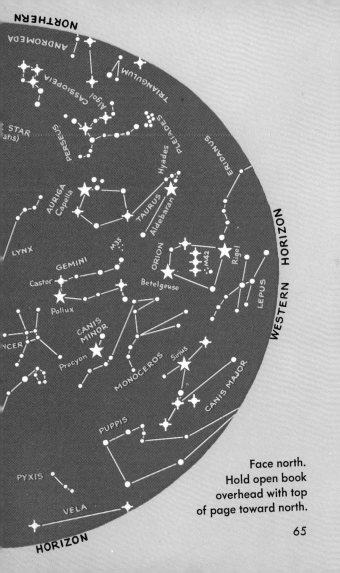

NORTHERN

ANDROMEDA

CASSIOPEIA

TRIANGULUM

Algol

PERSEUS

E STAR
(aris)

PLEIADES

ERIDANUS

Hyades

AURIGA
Capella

TAURUS
Aldebaran

WESTERN HORIZON

LYNX

M35

ORION

M42

Rigel

GEMINI

Castor

Betelgeuse

LEPUS

Pollux

CANIS
MINOR

NCER

Procyon

Sirius

MONOCEROS

CANIS MAJOR

PUPPIS

PYXIS

Face north.
Hold open book
overhead with top
of page toward north.

VELA

HORIZON

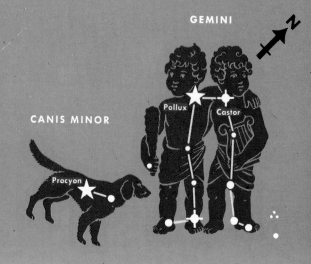

GEMINI, THE TWINS are often considered winter stars, though they are still high in the western sky at the first signs of spring. The bright stars Castor (2nd magnitude, white) and Pollux (1st magnitude, yellow), mark the Twins' heads. They are a scant 5 degrees apart, making good measuring points. Castor is a triple star, and each of its three components is a double star (six in all!). The bottom stars in the Big Dipper's bowl point in the direction of Castor. A line through Rigel and Betelgeuse in Orion points to Pollux. The cluster M35 in Gemini is worth locating with glasses.

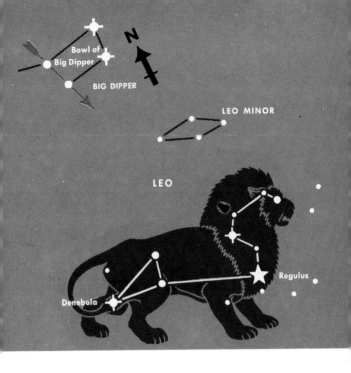

LEO, THE LION is the best known and most conspicious of the Zodiac constellations (pp. 100-101). The Sickle, or backwards question mark, which clearly forms the Lion's head, is found by following a line through the back stars of the Dipper's bowl southward. Regulus, a blue-white 1st-magnitude star, 86 light-years away, marks the base of the Sickle. The pointers of the Big Dipper point in one direction to the North Star; in the other direction, to the triangle that makes up the rear of Leo. The Leonid meteors radiate from this part of the sky in mid-November.

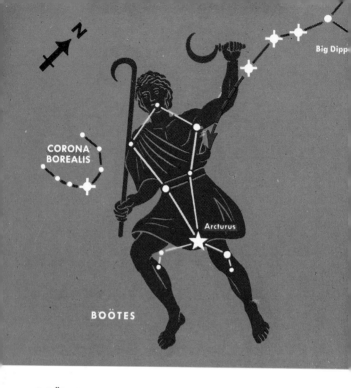

BOÖTES, THE HERDSMAN is found by following the curve of the handle of the Big Dipper 30 degrees to bright, orange Arcturus, a giant star 36 light-years away. The other stars in Boötes are of 3rd and 4th magnitude. Most of them form a kite-shaped figure extending close to the Dipper's handle. Boötes is chasing the Bears with a pair of Hunting Dogs, which make a small constellation between Arcturus and the Dipper's bowl. East of Boötes is the semicircular arc of stars forming Corona Borealis, the Northern Crown.

VIRGO, THE VIRGIN begins as a Y-shaped line of stars of 3rd and 4th magnitude extending toward Denebola, tail star of Leo. Spica ends this group; it is a blue-white, 1st-magnitude star 230 light-years away. The rest of Virgo is a line of three stars extending on from Spica, and a parallel line of three stars to the north. In Virgo is a cluster of several hundred galaxies about 14 million light-years away. A few of the brighter spiral nebulae can be seen with a small telescope. Follow the curve of the Dipper's handle through Arcturus to Spica.

69

CONSTELLATIONS OF SUMMER

As Leo sinks into the west, a number of new constellations and bright stars move up in the east. Summer is fine for watching them. The weather is likely to be favorable and you may have more leisure. The summer sky is not so brilliant as the early spring sky. You are not likely to see more than six 1st-magnitude stars. However, there are constellations aplenty, and the Milky Way is most impressive in summer.

Boötes, the Herdsman, a late spring constellation, is visible most of the summer, and Arcturus, found by following the curve of the Dipper's handle, is a good place to start exploring the summer sky. Rising just east of Boötes is the Northern Crown, Corona Borealis. Then to the south comes Libra, the Scales, a faint Zodiac constellation. Farther south and east of Libra is Scorpius, the Scorpion, marked by the red, 1st-magnitude star Antares. Moving north again you can trace out the thin line of Serpens, the Serpent, and Ophiuchus, the Serpent Bearer. The two constellations merge. A 2nd-magnitude star marks the head of Ophiuchus, but the remainder of both constellations are 3rd-, 4th-, and 5th-magnitude stars. This double star group has a midway position — midway between the pole and the equator and midway between the points where the sun appears on the first day of spring and fall. Still farther north is Hercules, about due east of the Crown.

East of Hercules is the "Summer Triangle" of 1st-magnitude stars set on the Milky Way. These are landmarks for the late summer sky, when they are nearly overhead. The three stars are Deneb in Cygnus, the Northern Cross; Vega in Lyra, the Lyre; and Altair in Aquila, the Eagle. Deneb is about 20 degrees east from Vega, and Altair is about 30 degrees from a line between them. South of Altair is Sagittarius, the Archer. Part of it forms the "Teapot." Near the triangle are small but bright Delphinus, the Dolphin, and Sagitta, the Arrow. The

southern summer sky in the region of Sagittarius is rich in star clusters and attractive faint stars.

ANGLES IN THE SKY Locating stars is easier if you estimate distances in degrees. A circle contains 360 degrees; the distance from the eastern to the western horizon through the zenith (overhead point) is 180 degrees. From horizon to zenith is 90 degrees. The pointers of the Big Dipper are about 5 degrees apart. From Denebola, at the tail of Leo, to the star at the top of the triangle is 10 degrees. From Rigel to Betelgeuse in Orion is 20 degrees. To avoid confusion as to which direction in the sky is north, which is east, and so on, refer to the Pole Star. Thus, to find Star A, 16 degrees "south" of Star B, draw an imaginary line from the Pole Star through Star B; then extend it 16 degrees. East and west are at right angles to this line. West is always the direction of a star's apparent motion as the evening progresses.

Any star can be exactly located on the celestial sphere by using the astronomical equivalents of latitude (declination) and longitude (right ascension). Star atlases are made on this basis. Large telescopes can be quickly directed toward a star whose position is known.

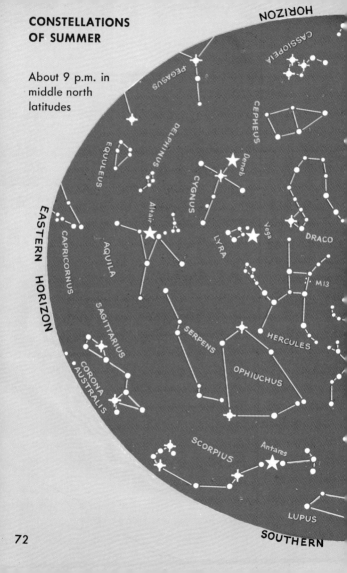

CONSTELLATIONS OF SUMMER

About 9 p.m. in middle north latitudes

HORIZON

CASSIOPEIA

PEGASUS

CEPHEUS

EQUULEUS

DELPHINUS

Deneb

CYGNUS

EASTERN HORIZON

CAPRICORNUS

Altair

Vega

LYRA

DRACO

AQUILA

M13

SAGITTARIUS

SERPENS

HERCULES

CORONA AUSTRALIS

OPHIUCHUS

SCORPIUS

Antares

LUPUS

72

SOUTHERN

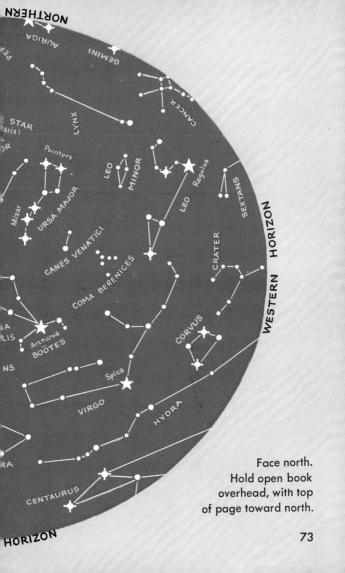

Face north.
Hold open book
overhead, with top
of page toward north.

HERCULES lies, upside down, just south of the head of Draco. A line from Arcturus to Deneb in the Northern Cross passes just north of it. A "keystone" of four 3rd- and 4th-magnitude stars marks the center of Hercules. Along its western edge is the famous cluster M13, 30,000 light-years away, with half a million stars. Through a telescope the cluster is a rare sight. The solar system is moving toward Hercules at 12 miles per second. However, because of the rotation of our galaxy, the net movement of the solar system is toward Cygnus.

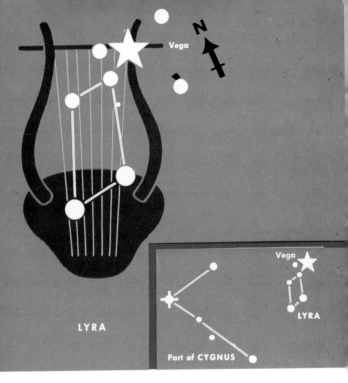

LYRA

Vega

N

Vega

LYRA

Part of CYGNUS

LYRA, THE LYRE is a small constellation marked by the splendor of Vega, its brightest star. Blue-white Vega, magnitude 0.1, 26 light-years away, is the brightest summer star. Between the pair of 3rd-magnitude stars at the end of the diamond-shaped constellation is the famed Ring Nebula, 5,400 light-years away (pp. 45-47). A large telescope is needed to see its details. One of the 3rd-magnitude stars in Lyra is a double star. The two stars eclipse every 13 days, the magnitude dropping from 3.4 to 4.3, then rising again.

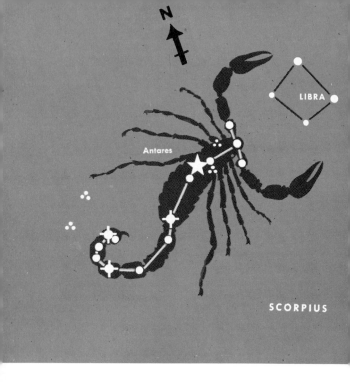

SCORPIUS, THE SCORPION   The fishhook shape of Scorpius in the southern sky is easy to identify. Antares, the red, 1st-magnitude star in the heart of the Scorpion, is a supergiant of a type that gives out much more light than other stars in the same spectral class. Antares' diameter is 390 times that of the sun, but its thin gases have a density of less than one-millionth of the sun's. It is 410 light-years away and has a faint green companion. Near Antares and between the tail of Scorpius and Sagittarius are several barely visible star clusters.

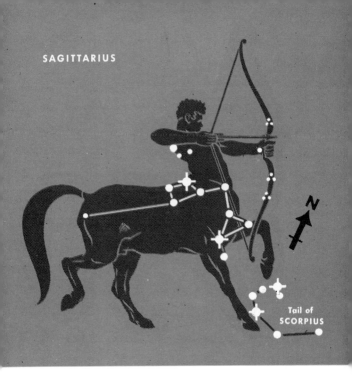

SAGITTARIUS

Tail of
SCORPIUS

SAGITTARIUS, THE ARCHER lies just east of Scorpius and follows it across the sky. Its central part is often called the "Teapot." Near the stars of the Archer's bow are several dark nebulae. The general region is rich in star clusters and nebulae. The Milky Way is brightest here for we are looking toward the center of our galaxy. A look at it with glasses or a telescope is exciting. According to myth, Sagittarius is shooting the Scorpion which stung Orion, the Hunter, causing his death. So Orion cannot be seen when Scorpius and Sagittarius are in the sky.

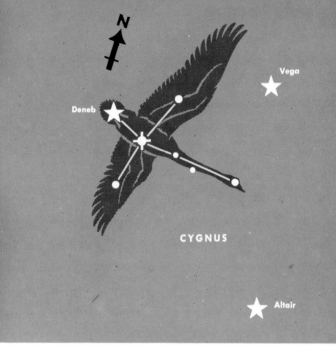

CYGNUS, THE SWAN is commonly called the Northern Cross and actually looks like a cross. Deneb, at the head of the Cross, is in the bright "Summer Triangle" with Altair in Aquila and Vega in Lyra. Albireo, a 3rd-magnitude double star, at the head of Cygnus, is almost on a line between Vega and Altair. The Milky Way splits here into parallel streams. The region is rich in varicolored stars — doubles and clusters. It is a region worth exploring. A 5th-magnitude star in Cygnus was the first star measured for distance. It is one of the nearest — 10.6 light-years away. The solar system is moving in this direction in the galaxy.

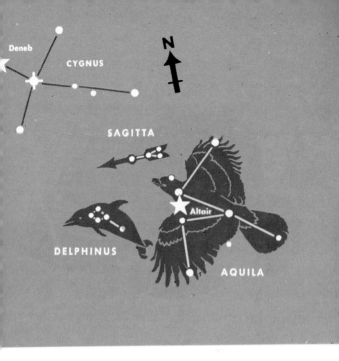

THE EAGLE, THE ARROW, and THE DOLPHIN are three neighboring constellations lying just south of the Cross and the Lyre. Aquila, the Eagle, is a large constellation. Most conspicuous in it is the bright star Altair (magnitude 0.8, distance 16 light-years) with a star on either side. The rest of the constellation makes a loose triangle pointed at Sagittarius. Sagitta, the Arrow, a faint but obvious constellation, lies between the Eagle and the Cross. Farther east and forming a triangle with Aquila and Sagitta is Delphinus, the Dolphin, or Job's Coffin, a small diamond of 4th-magnitude stars.

79

CONSTELLATIONS OF AUTUMN

Some of the autumn constellations follow so closely upon those labeled "summer" that they can be seen well before there is an autumn chill in the air. The autumn constellations are not quite equal to the brilliant skies of spring and summer. The constellation patterns overlap and hence are not so clear. The number of bright stars will entice the observer.

Four of the autumn constellations and two from the circumpolar group (p. 52) are drawn together by a famous Greek legend. No other legend is so well illustrated in constellations as that of the hero Perseus, the winged horse Pegasus, the king and queen of Ethiopia, and their fair daughter Andromeda. King Cepheus and his queen, Cassiopeia (both circumpolar constellations), lived happily until the queen offended the sea nymphs, who sent a sea monster (Cetus) to ravage the coast. The monster would depart only when the royal princess Andromeda was sacrificed. Andromeda was chained to a rock by the sea to await her doom. But just as the sea monster appeared, so did Perseus, the son of Jupiter, flying with winged sandals. Perseus was returning home from a perilous mission. He had just succeeded in killing the dreaded Medusa, a creature with such a terrifying face that mortals who gazed on her turned to stone. (From the blood of Medusa, Pegasus, the winged horse, had sprung.) After bargaining with the king, who promised his daughter to the hero if he saved her, Perseus slew the sea monster. Though the wedding feast was interrupted by a jealous suitor, the pair lived happily thereafter.

All the main characters of the Perseus legend are enshrined as constellations. Cetus, the Sea Monster, is a spreading constellation of dim stars. The five stars forming the head of Cetus lie in a rough circle southwest of the Pleiades and south of Andromeda. The constellation, extending south and west, has only one 2nd-magnitude star, but also includes a famous variable star, Mira.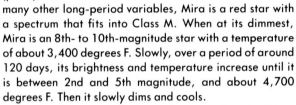

Mira is a long-period variable star (p. 39); it was discovered in 1596. Like many other long-period variables, Mira is a red star with a spectrum that fits into Class M. When at its dimmest, Mira is an 8th- to 10th-magnitude star with a temperature of about 3,400 degrees F. Slowly, over a period of around 120 days, its brightness and temperature increase until it is between 2nd and 5th magnitude, and about 4,700 degrees F. Then it slowly dims and cools.

Other minor constellations of autumn include Triangulum, the Triangle, a small group just south of Andromeda between Pegasus and Perseus. About 7 or 8 degrees southwest of the Triangle is Aries, the Ram. Look for a 2nd-, a 3rd-, and a 4th-magnitude star in a 5-degree curve. Pisces, the Fishes, a V-shaped group, fits around the southeast corner of the Square of Pegasus. The Northern Fish is a line of eight 4th- and 5th-magnitude stars. The Western Fish ends in a small circle of 5th- and 6th-magnitude stars just below the Square of Pegasus. Using the two western stars on the Square of Pegasus as pointers, extend a line south nearly 40 degrees and you may see a bright star (magnitude 1.2) close to the southern horizon. This is Fomalhaut, in the constellation of the Southern Fish. The rest of the constellation extends westward as a diamond-shaped group of 4th- and 5th-magnitude stars.

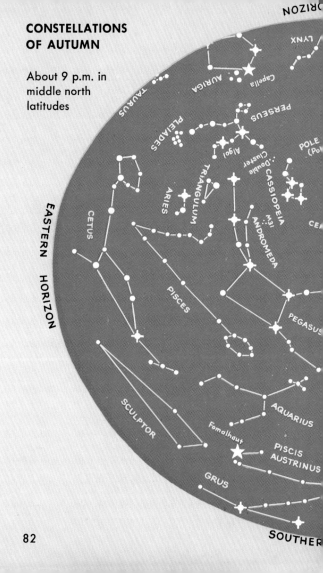

CONSTELLATIONS OF AUTUMN

About 9 p.m. in middle north latitudes

Capella

AURIGA

TAURUS

PERSEUS

PLEIADES

POLE
(Pol

Algol

CASSIOPEIA

Double
Cluster

M31

ANDROMEDA

CE

TRIANGULUM

ARIES

CETUS

EASTERN   HORIZON

PISCES

PEGASUS

SCULPTOR

AQUARIUS

Fomalhaut

PISCIS
AUSTRINUS

GRUS

82

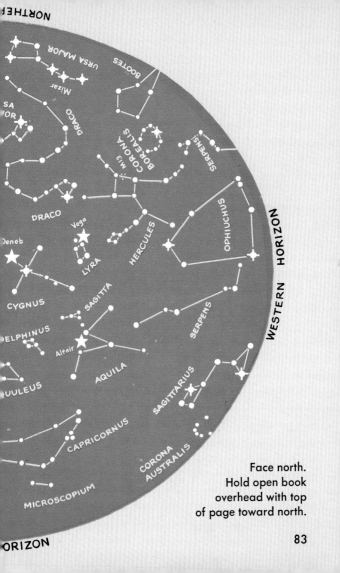

NORTHERN

URSA MAJOR

BOÖTES

Mizar

SA
OR

DRACO

CORONA
BOREALIS

SERPENS

M13

DRACO

Vega

HERCULES

OPHIUCHUS

Deneb

LYRA

CYGNUS

WESTERN HORIZON

DELPHINUS

SAGITTA

SERPENS

Altair

AQUILA

UUULEUS

SAGITTARIUS

CAPRICORNUS

CORONA
AUSTRALIS

Face north.
Hold open book
overhead with top
of page toward north.

MICROSCOPIUM

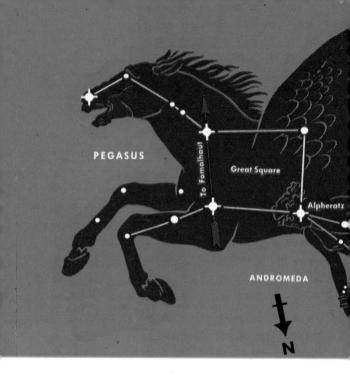

PEGASUS, THE WINGED HORSE is found by extending a line from the Pole Star through the west end of Cassiopeia. This line hits the eastern side of the great square — a rather imperfect square about 15 degrees on each side. West of the square the constellation extends toward Cygnus and Delphinus. Pegasus is upside down, with its head toward the equator. The 2nd-magnitude star Alpheratz, or Alpha Andromedae, is at the point where the constellations join. Pegasus was recorded as a constellation in ancient times.

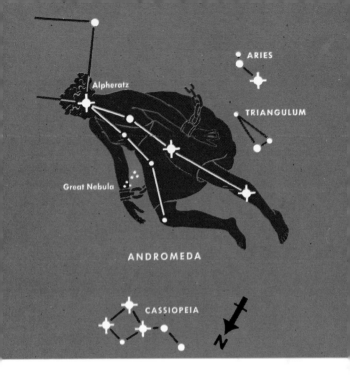

ANDROMEDA in chains extends eastward from Pegasus as two long, spreading lines of stars which meet at Alpheratz, a triple star (2.3, 5.4, and 6.6 magnitude). The northern line of stars extends toward Cassiopeia, the southern to Perseus. In Andromeda is Messier 31, the brightest and nearest of the spiral galaxies (pp. 42-43), visible to the naked eye (magnitude 5.0). It is about 2 million light-years away and has a diameter of about 150,000 light-years. This is how our galaxy would appear from this distance.

85

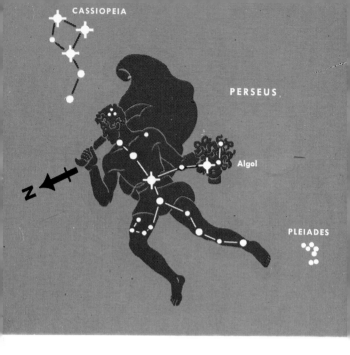

PERSEUS lies close to Cassiopeia. A curved line of stars forming part of Perseus extends toward Auriga. Other stars in Perseus complete its rough, K-shaped figure. The downward side of the K points to the Pleiades. The upward arm ends with Algol, best known of the eclipsing binary variable stars — the "Demon Star," or head of Medusa. The brighter star is three times the diameter of our sun; the dimmer, even larger. As they revolve, about 13 million miles apart, the dim star eclipses the bright star once every three days, causing a five-hour long drop from 2.3 magnitude to 3.4; over the next 5 hours it brightens again.

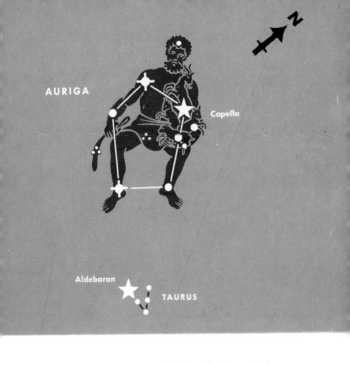

AURIGA, THE CHARIOTEER is the last of the autumn constellations, heralding the coming winter. Auriga lies to the east of Perseus. A line drawn from the top stars of the Big Dipper's bowl points close to Capella, a bright triple star (magnitude 0.1), farthest north of the 1st-magnitude stars. Capella is sometimes known as The Goat; a nearby triangle of stars are the Kids. Several open clusters (M37 and M38 especially) are found in Auriga. Each contains about 100 stars and is about 2,700 light-years away. The main part of Auriga is a five-sided figure of 1st-, 2nd-, and 3rd-magnitude stars.

CONSTELLATIONS OF WINTER

The sky is never clearer than on cold, sparkling winter nights. It is at those times that the fainter stars are seen in great profusion. Then the careful observer can pick out dim borderline stars and nebulae that cannot be seen when the air is less clear. The winter constellations include some of the brightest and easiest to recognize. Eight 1st-magnitude stars are visible on January evenings, and you may see up to 11 by early spring.

For the watcher of these faint stars the period of accommodation, or getting used to the dark, is important. You will need at least 5 or 10 minutes after looking at a bright light before your eyes will once again see the faintest stars. Use your star map first and then do your observation. If you use a flashlight while observing, cover the lens with red cellophane or with a sheet of thin paper to cut down the intensity of the light. Another good trick in viewing faint stars is to look a bit to one side and not directly at them. This side vision is actually more sensitive than direct vision.

The winter constellations center about Orion, the Hunter, who according to the Greek myths boasted that no animal could overcome him. Jupiter sent a scorpion which bit Orion in the heel, killing him. When Orion was placed in the sky, with his two hunting dogs and the hare he was chasing, the scorpion that stung him was placed there too, but on the opposite side of the heavens.

The winter skies also include Taurus, the Bull, of which the Pleiades are a part, and some minor star groups.

Use Orion, so clear and easy to find in the winter sky, as a key to other nearby constellations (see p. 94). The belt of Orion acts as a pointer in two directions. To the northwest, it points toward Aldebaran in Taurus, the Bull,

and on, past Aldebaran, toward the Pleiades. In the opposite direction, the belt of Orion points toward Sirius, the Dog Star. Sirius, Procyon (the Little Dog), and Betelgeuse in Orion form a triangle with equal sides about 25 degrees long. South of Orion, about 10 degrees, is Lepus, the Hare; and another 15 degrees south is Columba the Dove (p. 96). A line from Rigel through Betelgeuse points roughly in the direction of Gemini, the Twins.

With such stars as Betelgeuse, Aldebaran, and Rigel in the winter sky, it is worth recalling that these represent an Arabian contribution to astronomy from the 8th to the 12th century. Arabian star names are common. The Greeks, Romans, and their western European descendants gave names to the constellations, most of which represent characters from Greek and Roman myths. Some of the star names are from the Latin, too. Many of the ideas developed by the early astronomers have been discarded, as the limited observations of those days led to incomplete or wrong interpretations. But the names given to stars and constellations have often remained unchanged for centuries and are as useful now as they were long ago.

Because winter nights are long, and often clear, they offer an excellent opportunity for photographing stars and planets. The books listed on p. 11 will tell you more about this interesting hobby. Star trails and photos showing the movement of the moon or other planets can be made with no equipment other than a camera. For other kinds of photographs of heavenly bodies, a polar axis, motor-driven with a clock, is needed to keep the camera accurately following the star or planet.

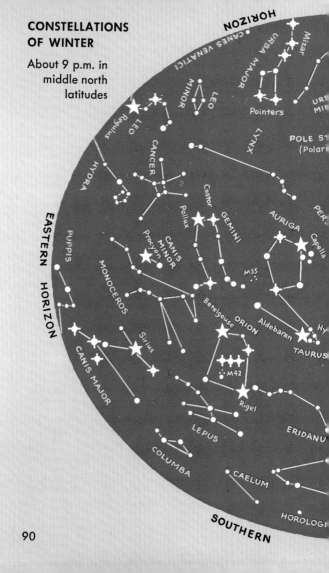

CONSTELLATIONS OF WINTER

About 9 p.m. in middle north latitudes

HORIZON

CANES VENATICI

URSA MAJOR

Mizar

URSA MINOR

Pointers

LEO MINOR

LEO

Regulus

LYNX

POLE STAR
(Polaris)

HYDRA

CANCER

GEMINI

Castor

Pollux

AURIGA

PER.

EASTERN

PUPPIS

CANIS MINOR

Procyon

M35

Capella

MONOCEROS

Betelgeuse

ORION

Aldebaran

HORIZON

Sirius

Hy

TAURUS

CANIS MAJOR

M42

Rigel

LEPUS

ERIDANU

COLUMBA

CAELUM

HOROLOG

SOUTHERN

90

NORTHERN

DRACO

CYGNUS

Deneb

CEPHEUS

PEGASUS

CASSIOPEIA

M 31

ANDROMEDA

AQUARIUS

Algol

TRIANGULUM

PISCES

PLEIADES   ARIES

SCULPTOR

CETUS

PHOENIX

FORNAX

WESTERN HORIZON

Face north.
Hold open book
overhead with top
of page toward north.

HORIZON

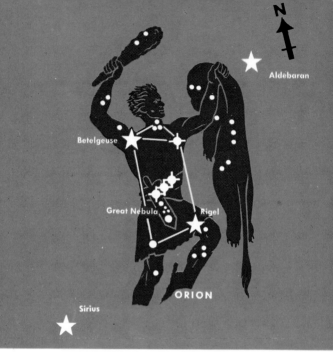

ORION, THE HUNTER is conspicuous and easily remembered. A line drawn from Polaris through Capella in Auriga will bring you to Orion. So will a line from the stars forming the ends of the horns of Taurus, the Bull. The rectangle forming the Hunter's torso is bounded by bright stars. Betelgeuse is a red variable supergiant (magnitude 0.7). Rigel, diagonally opposite but blue-white, is a supergiant double (magnitude 0.1). From Orion's belt, 3 degrees long, hangs the faint sword, containing the great nebula M42, a mass of glowing gas 26 light-years in diameter and 1,625 light-years away.

92

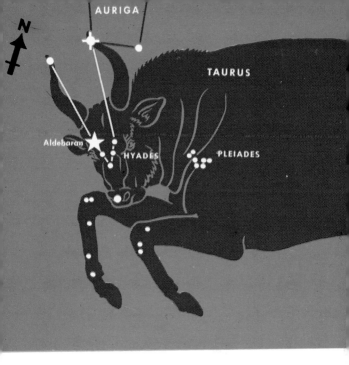

TAURUS, THE BULL represents the form Jupiter took to carry off Europa, a young princess. (Only the forepart of the Bull got into the sky.) Most conspicuous stars in Taurus are the Hyades, which form its face. This clear, V-shaped star group has Aldebaran, a red 1st-magnitude star, at one end. Aldebaran is a double star 68 light-years away. The Hyades, actually a loose cluster of about 150 stars, are about 120 light-years away. From them extend the horns of Taurus. The 2nd-magnitude star El Nath, forming the tip of the Northern Horn, is also part of Auriga and can serve as a guide to Taurus.

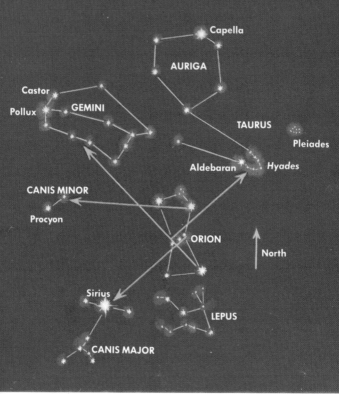

Orion as a Guide to Winter Constellations

THE WINTER SKY sparkles with bright stars. A good guide is to use Orion as a pointer to other constellations. The belt points southeast to Sirius and Canis Major, northwest to Aldebaran and Taurus. These lead on to other star groups.

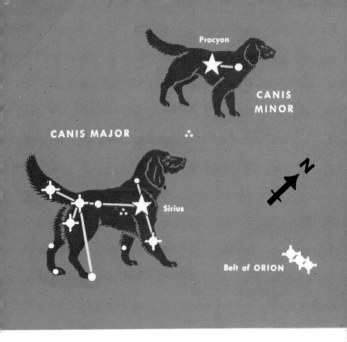

CANIS MAJOR AND MINOR are two constellations, each of which has a major star. In Canis Major (the Big Dog), Sirius, brightest of all stars, dominates. With a magnitude of -1.43 it is over 300 times brighter than the faintest visible stars. Sirius, the Dog Star, is only 8.8 light-years away. The rest of Canis Major includes double and triple stars and several clusters. Canis Minor, the Little Dog, is smaller and has only one visible star besides Procyon (magnitude 0.4). The belt of Orion points eastward and a little south to Sirius. An eastward line from Betelgeuse in Orion takes you to Procyon.

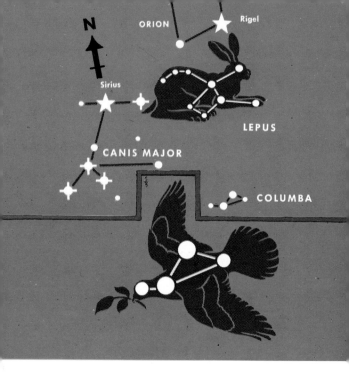

LEPUS, THE HARE and COLUMBA, THE DOVE are small, faint constellations near Orion. Lepus is south of Orion and due west of Canis Major. The main part of the constellation is a four-sided figure of 3rd- and 4th-magnitude stars. Most of the other stars are between this group and Orion. The Dove, which commemorates the dove which flew out from Noah's Ark, is an even smaller constellation south of Lepus and, in most parts of the United States, close to the southern horizon. The four stars form a close group about 5 degrees long.

SOUTHERN HEMISPHERE CONSTELLATIONS

The farther south you go, the more southern stars you can see. At 40 degrees N. latitude about half the southern stars are visible. In southern Florida and Texas the Southern Cross is seen. Southern constellations not thus far described are in a circle (next page) within 40 degrees from the South Pole. They were described first by Magellan and other early observers. Most famous is the Southern Cross, 6 degrees long, pointing to the South Pole. The Centaur, nearby, has two 1st-magnitude stars. A companion to one of them is the nearest star to the earth. The Magellanic Clouds are close companions of our galaxy.

Right: Strip of Sky from North Pole to South Pole

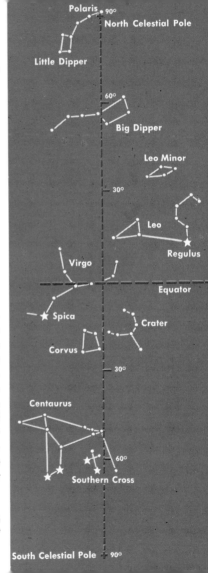

Polaris 90°
North Celestial Pole
Little Dipper
60°
Big Dipper
Leo Minor
30°
Leo
Regulus
Virgo
Equator
Spica
Crater
Corvus
30°
Centaurus
60°
Southern Cross
South Celestial Pole 90°

SOUTH CIRCUMPOLAR CONSTELLATIONS

At about 40 degrees south latitude the following are the chief circumpolar constellations: Crux (Southern Cross), Carina (the Keel, of the ship Argo), Volans (Flying Fish), Dorado (Goldfish or Swordfish), Hydrus (Small Water Snake), Tucana (Toucan), Octans (Octant), Pavo (Peacock), Ara (Altar), Triangulum Australe (Southern Triangle), and Centaurus (Centaur).

At about the equator you can locate these constellations with the accompanying chart. Facing south, hold the open book in front of you so that the current month is toward the top. The constellations are now about as you will see them during the current month at 9 p.m. To see how they will appear earlier, turn the chart counterclockwise; for a later time, clockwise. A quarter of a turn shows a six-hour change.

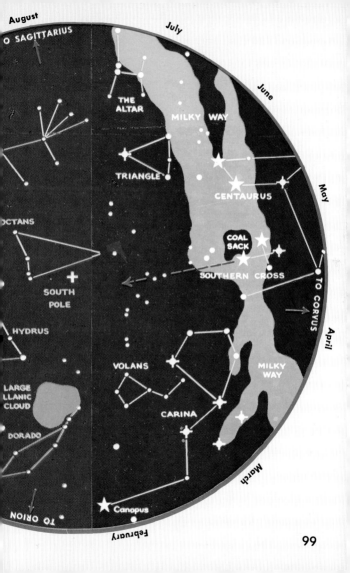

99

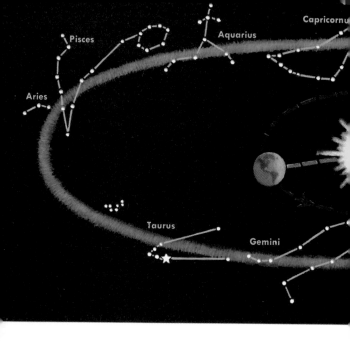

THE ZODIAC is a belt of 12 constellations: Aries, Taurus, Gemini, Cancer, Leo, Virgo, Libra, Scorpius, Sagittarius, Capricornus, Aquarius, Pisces. These star groups circle the sky close to the ecliptic, which is the great circle of the earth's orbit around the sun. The sun, moon, and planets look as though they move against the background of these constellations and seem to be "in" them. Easiest to observe is the moon's path. The journeys of the planets take longer, depending on their distance from the sun.

The sun itself seems to move through the Zodiac constellations each year along the line called the ecliptic. The change of constellations seen just before sunrise or after

100

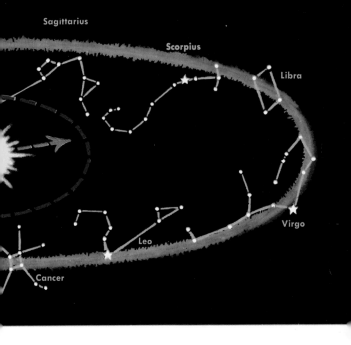

sunset confirms this movement. Note, in the diagram, the earth circling the sun. From the earth, the sun seems to be in the constellation Libra. As the earth revolves, the sun will seem to move through Scorpius and Sagittarius, until finally it is back in Libra again.

Babylonians and other ancient astronomers recognized this apparent motion of the sun, moon, and planets. This knowledge helped them predict the seasons. Nowadays the Zodiac is often linked to astrology, which claims to interpret the influence of stars on people and worldly events. Astronomers are convinced that astrology has no scientific foundation.

101

Sun

Mercury

Venus

Earth

Mars

THE SOLAR SYSTEM

There are altogether in the sun's family 9 major planets, more than 4 dozen moons or satellites, hundreds of thousands of minor planets or asteroids, billions of comets, and untold millions of meteoroids. Central star of the solar system, the sun makes up over 99 percent of its mass (weight).

The planets range from tiny Mercury, which is some 36 million miles from the sun, to farthest (and smallest) Pluto. Mercury goes around the sun in three earth-months. Pluto takes almost 250 earth-years to circle the sun once.

Around some of the planets revolve moons. Although Mercury and Venus have none, the other planets have from one to more than a dozen. Jupiter, the largest planet, has at least 16, and Saturn has at least 17. Four of Jupiter's satellites can be seen with field glasses or a small telescope.

The rings of Saturn, made of millions of tiny fragments, can be seen in a small telescope as a platelike belt around the planet. Uranus also has rings.

Most asteroids revolve in paths between Mars and Jupiter. The brighter ones can be found by amateurs with telescopes if their positions are known.

Comets, circling the sun in elongated orbits, cruise into view and out again in periods ranging from a few years to several hundred years and much longer.

Meteors, which appear as bright streaks or flashes in

Jupiter

Saturn

Uranus

Neptune

Pluto

the sky, burn because of friction with the earth's atmosphere. Meteorites that strike the earth provide material from outer space that one can study first hand. Only on earth is life definitely known to exist. Temperatures on the other planets are probably too extreme to permit plant or animal life as we know it. Planets beyond Pluto may exist.

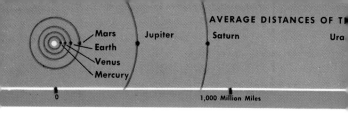

THE PLANETS

	Mercury	Venus	Earth
Average distance from sun (in millions of miles)	36	67	93
Distance from sun (compared to earth)	0.39	0.72	1.00
Diameter at equator (in miles)	3,030	7,518	7,923
Mass or weight (compared to earth)	0.06	0.82	1.00
Volume (compared to earth)	0.06	0.92	1.00
Number of moons	0	0	1
Length of day (in hours)	1,408	5,832	24
Length of year (compared to earth)	0.24	0.62	1.00
Inclination of equator to orbit (in degrees)	0	177	23.5
Weight of an object weighing 100 lbs. on earth (in pounds)	38	90	100

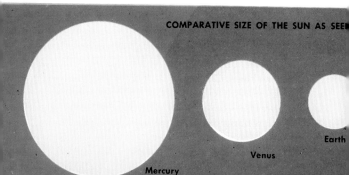

COMPARATIVE SIZE OF THE SUN AS SEE█

Neptune   Pluto

0 Million Miles   3,000 Million Miles

Mars	Jupiter	Saturn	Uranus	Neptune	Pluto
142	483	886	1,782	2,793	3,670
1.52	5.20	9.54	19.18	30.06	39.44
4,219	88,012	74,500	31,550	30,190	1,860(?)
0.11	317.9	95.2	14.6	17.2	0.002(?)
0.15	1,318	736	64	60	0.01
2	16	17	15	2	1
24.6	9.8	10.2	16.8	17.8	153
1.9	12	29	84	165	248
25	3.1	26.7	98	30	118(?)
38	287	132	93	123	3(?)

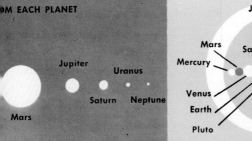

OM EACH PLANET

Mars   Jupiter   Saturn   Uranus   Neptune

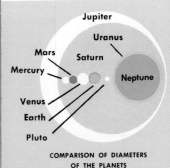

Jupiter
Uranus
Mars   Saturn
Mercury   Neptune
Venus
Earth
Pluto

COMPARISON OF DIAMETERS
OF THE PLANETS

Early Theory of Origin of Solar System

ORIGIN OF THE SOLAR SYSTEM   Any theory that tries
to explain how our sun and planets came to be the way
they are must account for several things: All the planets
revolve about the sun in nearly circular orbits in the same
direction, nearly in the same plane; the sun slowly rotates
on its axis in the same direction; all but two of the planets
(Venus and Uranus) rotate on their axes in the same direction; the inner planets are largely rocky with relatively thin
atmospheres, while the outer planets have extensive atmospheres and are mostly gas; the largest planets are
neither the closest nor the farthest from the sun.

About 5 billion years ago, something, perhaps a nearby
supernova explosion, caused a cloud of interstellar gas to
begin contracting, heating up, and separating into a dense

inner region and a diffuse outer region. The inner region shrank further to become the sun. Within the cloud, dust grains and gas molecules collided and stuck together. Close to the proto-sun the temperature was hot enough to boil away gases leaving rocky material; in the outer parts of the cloud it was too cool and so the gases remained. As the sun finally became an adult star, a burst of light and solar particles blew away the remaining gas. The atmospheres of the inner planets came from gases from the rocks.

Planetary systems may exist around other stars, though none have been detected for certain. It is possible that life evolved on some of them. The new space telescope will be able to detect Jupiter-sized planets around the nearest stars, if there are any.

Stages in the Formation of the Solar System

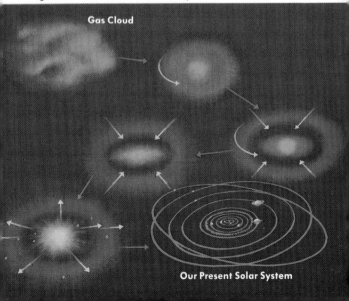

Gas Cloud

Our Present Solar System

Mercury Photographed by the Mariner 10 Spacecraft   NASA

MERCURY, the planet that is the nearest to the sun, can at times be seen in the east just before sunrise or in the west just after sunset. It has phases like the moon's (p. 140). Mercury revolves about the sun every 88 days in an eccentric orbit and rotates on its axis every 58 or 59 days. The direction of rotation is from west to east. The same side of Mercury does not always face the sun, as once believed. Spacecraft have photographed most of Mercury's surface.

Venus Photographed by the Mariner 10 Spacecraft   NASA

VENUS, called the Morning or Evening Star depending on when it is visible, is the nearest of the principal planets — about 26 million miles away at its closest approach. Then it appears through the telescope as a thin crescent. It is brightest a month later — 15 times brighter than Sirius, the brightest star. A dense acidic atmosphere conceals the planet's surface, and its surface temperature is over 900° F. It rotates from east to west.

EARTH, the planet on which we live, gives a basis for understanding the others. The earth has been accurately measured. Its diameter at the equator is 7,926.38 miles; through the poles it is only 7,899.81 miles, or 26.6 miles less. This very slight flattening at the poles leaves the earth an almost perfect sphere. An atmosphere of gases surrounds the earth, extending upward about 500 miles. But the atmosphere decreases rapidly with altitude, becoming thinner and thinner as one goes higher. Half of it is found within 3 miles of the surface. The atmosphere is an essential part of such effects as rainbows, sunrise and sunset colors, and auroras. The atmosphere formed early in earth's evolution by gases from the planet's interior.

The earth has a complex pattern of motions, all of which affect our relationship to the stars and other planets. First, the earth rotates on its axis in four minutes less than 24 hours as measured by your watch. Second, the earth revolves on its 600-million mile orbit around the sun once a year, at a speed of 18½ miles per second. Third, the earth's axis has a motion, called precession (p.53), making one turn in about 26,000 years. Fourth, the North and South Poles are not stationary, but wander in rough circles about 40 feet in diameter. Finally, there is a solar motion of about 12 miles per second, while our part of the galaxy seems to be whirling through space at 170 miles per second.

The weight of the earth is written as 66 followed by 20 zeros tons. On the average, it is 5½ times as heavy as an equal-sized body of water. However, studies of rock, of earthquake waves, and of gravity show that the earth is not the same throughout. Near the center of the earth the material is under pressure of about 25,000 tons per square inch. That tremendous pressure creates a very dense core averaging about 10 to 12 times the weight of water. From the center of the earth to the surface is about 3,950 miles.

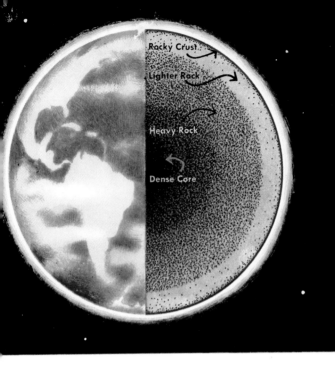

The first 2,200 is the dense, heavy, partially liquid compressed rock. The pressure causes this core to react like a liquid to earthquake waves.

Surrounding the core is a 1,700-mile rigid layer of heavy rock which grades off into lighter rocks nearer the surface. Finally comes the outer rocky crust, up to 25 miles thick, where the density of the rock has been altered into soil by the action of water and air. It is here that life is concentrated.

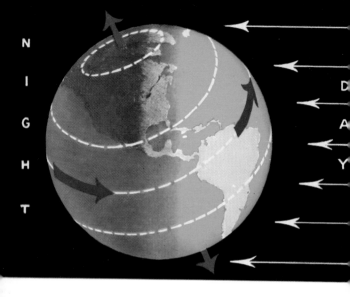

DAY AND NIGHT are due to the earth's rotation. The earth is a dark sphere lighted on one side by the sun. As the earth rotates on its axis from west to east every 24 hours, the sun seems to rise in the east, cross the sky, and set in the west. The earth's atmosphere bends and diffuses the sunlight, before the sun rises, to make dawn, and it keeps the sky light for a time after the sun has set. Day and night are always equal at the equator, but because of the tilting of the earth's axis to the plane of its orbit, only about the first days of spring and fall are day and night equal in middle latitudes. In the Northern Hemisphere, length of daylight and height of the sun above the horizon at noon increase from the first day of winter to the first day of summer, then decrease again. The polar regions have 24-hour days during summer.

112

TIME The earth rotates through 360 degrees in about 24 hours, at the rate of 15 degrees per hour. New York City and Lima, Peru, have the same sun-time, because they have the same longitude. But when it is noon in New York it is still late morning in Chicago.

When the sun reaches its highest point (noon) at a given location, the time at a point 15 degrees west of that location is only 11 o'clock. Local time is therefore different for all places that are not on the same longitude. When only local time was used, New York clocks were 11½ minutes behind Boston, and Washington's were 12½ minutes behind New York. To avoid the confusion resulting from such small differences, in 1883 the nation was divided into time zones, each about 15 degrees wide and each differing by one hour in time. Similar zones now girdle the earth — 24 of them.

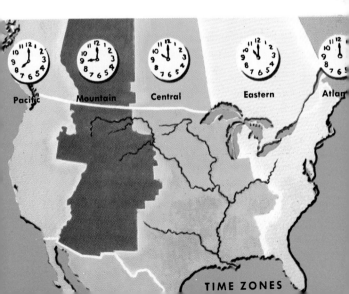

Pacific   Mountain   Central   Eastern   Atlan

TIME ZONES

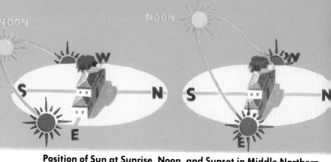

Position of Sun at Sunrise, Noon, and Sunset in Middle Northern

EARTH SEASONS Because of the 23½-degree tilt of the earth's axis, the sun is above the horizon for different lengths of time at different seasons. The tilt determines whether the sun's rays strike us at a low angle or more directly. At New York's latitude the more nearly direct rays on June 22 bring about three times as much heat as the more slanting rays of December 22. Heat received by any region depends on length of daylight and angle of the sun above the horizon. Hence the differences in seasons in different parts of the world.

In the region within 23½ degrees of the poles, the sun remains above the horizon 24 hours a day during some part of the summer. The farther north, the longer it stays above the horizon. Every place above the Arctic Circle experiences the midnight sun. In the area within 23½ degrees of the equator, the sun is overhead at noon at some time during summer. For latitudes in between, the highest point reached by the sun in summer is 90 degrees minus the latitude, plus 23½ degrees. The low point of the noonday

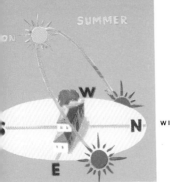

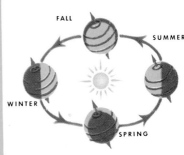

SUMMER

FALL

SUMMER

WINTER

SPRING

Latitudes at Beginning of Each Season

sun, in midwinter, is 90 minus the latitude, minus 23½ degrees. At Chicago (latitude 42 degrees north) the height of the noonday sun varies from 24 degrees in winter to 71½ degrees in summer.

Local conditions affect seasonal patterns. Mountain ranges, ocean currents, altitude, prevailing winds, and other factors produce the seasonal climate in a given locality. But the angle of the sun's rays is still a most important factor in determining the plant, animal, and human life in a region.

Positions of Midnight Sun at 15-Minute Intervals above the Arctic Circle

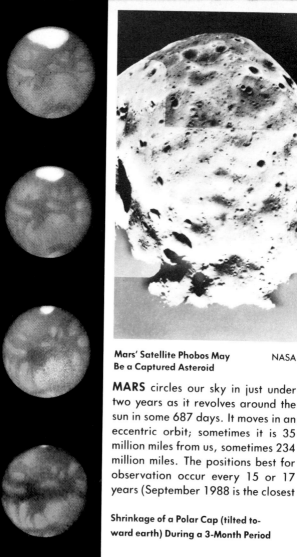

Mars' Satellite Phobos May Be a Captured Asteroid   NASA

MARS circles our sky in just under two years as it revolves around the sun in some 687 days. It moves in an eccentric orbit; sometimes it is 35 million miles from us, sometimes 234 million miles. The positions best for observation occur every 15 or 17 years (September 1988 is the closest

Shrinkage of a Polar Cap (tilted toward earth) During a 3-Month Period

Mars' Surface in Winter, Photographed by the Viking Lander   NASA

such time). Flybys of Mars by Mariner probes showed the surface to be covered by craters, created by asteroidal impact, ranging from several hundred miles to a thousand feet. The surface shows a striking similarity to the moon. No canals were found. The reported canals of the past century's observations were made up of unrelated dark spots put together as continuous features by the observer's eye and mind. The polar caps are real and probably are made up of a mixture of snow and dry ice. The atmosphere is largely carbon dioxide. Temperatures may reach 60°F in the daytime and −100°F at night.

JUPITER is the largest planet. It never comes closer than 367 million miles to earth, and it takes 12 of our years to orbit the the sun. Its solid surface lies thousands of miles below the cloudtops that we see. Jupiter rotates in less than 10 hours, the fastest of any planet.

The atmosphere is mostly very cold hydrogen and helium, and the clouds are methane and ammonia, arranged in belts and bands parallel to Jupiter's equator. The clouds are in violent swirling motion. Some larger features, such as the Great Red Spot, persist for centuries; it is 30,000 miles long, large enough to drop the earth in.

Jupiter is orbited by a retinue of satellites, almost a mini-solar system of its own. Four of these are bright enough to be seen with field glasses, with diameters ranging from 1,900 to 3,200 miles. They were discovered in 1610 by Galileo, and so are called the Galilean Satellites: Io, Europa, Ganymede, and Callisto. They often pass in front of or behind Jupiter as seen from earth. Io is the most volcanic object in the solar system, spewing out fountains of molten sulfur. Europa may have liquid water under its solid crust of ice and rock. Some of the satellites show evidence of bombardment by meteoroids. The smaller satellites were discovered by the Voyager spacecraft. The outer ones are probably captured asteroids.

Jupiter also has a faint ring, not visible except with special instruments, and an extremely strong magnetic field with swarms of atomic particles captured in radiation belts.

Right: Jupiter and Four of Its Satellites. Top Left: Io; Bottom Left: Ganymede; Center: Europa; Bottom Right: Callisto   NASA

SATURN is the most distant of the planets visible to the unaided eye, although it takes a telescope to see the famous rings. Orbiting the sun every 29 years, it never gets closer than 745 million miles. Saturn has a day only about 10 hours long.

Saturn's atmosphere is, like Jupiter's, mostly very cold hydrogen and helium. Being farther away from the sun, it is colder, the bands are less colorful, and the features more permanent. Saturn may have no solid surface below the clouds. Its density is so low that it would float if you could find a body of water large enough to float it in.

The rings, discovered by telescope in 1655, are small particles of ice and rock that never collected to become a satellite. There are three major rings, and many more minor ones. Visible from earth are a bright outer ring, then a thin dark band called "Cassini's Division," then the broadest bright ring, another gap, and a faint inner "crepe" ring. The rings are hundreds of thousands of miles across, but less than a mile thick, so stars and Saturn's surface can be seen through them.

Saturn has a large family of satellites, a few of them visible in small telescopes. The largest is Titan, the only satellite in the solar system to have an atmosphere. Mimas, the innermost moon, has a crater covering almost a quarter of its own diameter. All the others are also heavily cratered from meteoroid hits. There are at least 17 satellites, and probably many more very tiny ones not yet discovered. Several of the smaller ones were found in photographs taken by the Voyager spacecraft.

Right: Saturn and Six of Its Satellites. Top to Bottom: Titan, Mimas, Tethys, Dione, Rhea, Enceladus
NASA

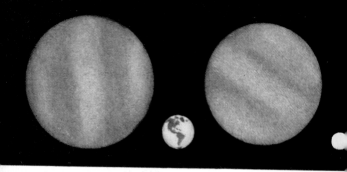

Left to Right: Uranus, Earth, Neptune, Pluto

Photographic Plates by Which Pluto Was Discovered (note arrows)

URANUS, NEPTUNE, and PLUTO Uranus may be seen by a sharp-eyed observer. The other outer planets are telescopic. Uranus was accidentally discovered in 1781. Its failure to follow its predicted orbit seemed to be due to the gravitational pull of a planet farther out. Two astronomers independently calculated the position of the undiscovered planet, and when telescopes were turned to this region in 1846, Neptune was found. Pluto, the smallest planet, was discovered in 1930 at the Lowell Observatory as the successful conclusion of a search over many years.

View from Outer Space of Asteroids Between Mars and Jupiter

ASTEROIDS   The minor planets are all telescopic objects. Most of them were discovered photographically. About 1,800 have names and there are probably hundreds of thousands more. The largest, Ceres, has a diameter of 480 miles. Most of the rest are less than 50 miles wide. The majority move between the orbits of Mars and Jupiter. Others enter the area between Mars and the sun. Some come within a few million miles of earth. Mars' satellites (p. 116) and Jupiter's outer satellites may be captured asteroids.

123

LOCATING THE VISIBLE PLANETS

The table here will help you locate the best-known planets in the constellations where they will be at various times. The constellations are those of the Zodiac (pp. 100-101). Positions are approximate. To be sure of not mistaking a star for a planet, check appropriate constellation charts if necessary. Another clue is that planets, when high in the sky, usually do not twinkle, while stars sometimes do.

For positions of Mercury, which is visible to the unaided eye but hard to spot, and Uranus, Neptune, and Pluto, which require a telescope, consult astronomy magazines, *The Observer's Handbook* from the Royal Astronomical Society of Canada, or other yearly astronomical handbooks often available in local planetarium book stores.

Italic type indicates the planet is a morning star, rising before the sun; regular type indicates an evening star, appearing after sunset. Dashes indicate planet is too close to the sun for visibility. Adapted from *Skyguide*, where more complete tables can be found.

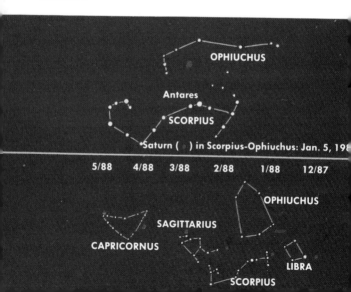

Year	Month	Venus	Mars	Jupiter	Saturn
1985	Jan	Aquarius	Aquarius	Sagittarius	*Libra*
	Apr	—	Aries	Capricornus	*Libra*
	Jul	*Taurus*	—	Capricornus	*Libra*
	Oct	*Leo*	Leo	Capricornus	*Libra*
1986	Jan	—	*Libra*	Capricornus	*Scorpius*
	Apr	Aries	*Sagittarius*	Aquarius	*Scorpius*
	Jul	Leo	Sagittarius	Pisces	*Scorpius*
	Oct	Libra	Sagittarius	Aquarius	*Scorpius*
1987	Jan	*Libra*	Pisces	Aquarius	*Scorpius*
	Apr	*Aquarius*	Taurus	Pisces	*Sagittarius*
	Jul	*Taurus*	Cancer	Pisces	*Scorpius*
	Oct	Virgo	*Virgo*	Pisces	*Scorpius*
1988	Jan	Capricornus	*Scorpius*	Pisces	*Sagittarius*
	Apr	*Taurus*	*Capricornus*	Aries	*Sagittarius*
	Jul	*Taurus*	Pisces	*Taurus*	*Sagittarius*
	Oct	*Leo*	Pisces	*Taurus*	*Sagittarius*
1989	Jan	*Sagittarius*	Pisces	Taurus	*Sagittarius*
	Apr	—	Taurus	Taurus	*Sagittarius*
	Jul	Cancer	Cancer	*Taurus*	*Sagittarius*
	Oct	Scorpius	—	Gemini	*Sagittarius*

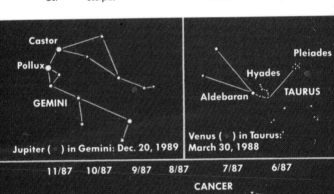

Jupiter ( ) in Gemini: Dec. 20, 1989

Venus ( ) in Taurus: March 30, 1988

Path of Mars ( ): June 1987–May 1988

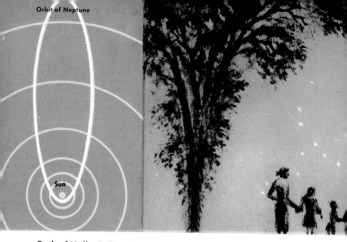

Orbit of Neptune

Sun

Path of Halley's Comet

HALLEY'S COMET is the most famous example of these unusual members of the solar system. Comet Halley has been observed since at least 240 B.C., and returns to the vicinity of earth every 76 years. Its very elongated orbit takes it beyond the orbit of Neptune, and within the orbit of Mercury.

The most recent previous appearance of this comet was in May of 1910. At that time the head passed within a few million miles of earth, and our planet actually went through the comet's thin tail, with no ill effects. The wispy tail could be seen arcing across the sky.

This time the comet will not come very close to earth, for our planet will be on the far side of the sun from where Halley crosses our orbit. This means that it will not be nearly as bright as it was in 1910. Although it is now within range of telescopes, in late 1985 it will become visible with binoculars and possibly by the unaided eye in good conditions.

126

Halley's Comet, Morning of May 13, 1910

After passing closest to the sun in February 1986, Halley should be visible to the unaided eye in the spring of that year, gradually disappearing by summertime. It will remain visible in telescopes for several years.

Halley will be visible best in the Southern Hemisphere, but it will also be visible north of the equator. It can be

seen in the evening sky after sunset in January 1986, and again in late April; in March it will be in the eastern sky before dawn. The tail will be of greatest length (as seen from earth) in late March-early April.

Effect of Sun's Rays on Tail of Comet

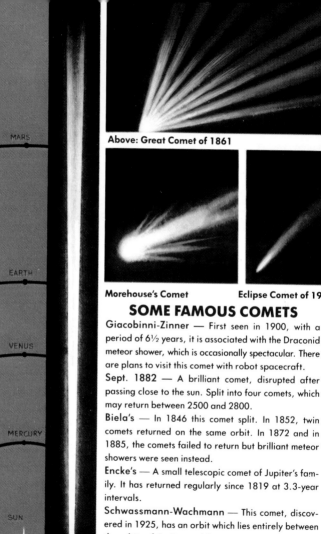

Above: Great Comet of 1861

Morehouse's Comet   Eclipse Comet of 1948

SOME FAMOUS COMETS

Giacobinni-Zinner — First seen in 1900, with a period of 6½ years, it is associated with the Draconid meteor shower, which is occasionally spectacular. There are plans to visit this comet with robot spacecraft.

Sept. 1882 — A brilliant comet, disrupted after passing close to the sun. Split into four comets, which may return between 2500 and 2800.

Biela's — In 1846 this comet split. In 1852, twin comets returned on the same orbit. In 1872 and in 1885, the comets failed to return but brilliant meteor showers were seen instead.

Encke's — A small telescopic comet of Jupiter's family. It has returned regularly since 1819 at 3.3-year intervals.

Schwassmann-Wachmann — This comet, discovered in 1925, has an orbit which lies entirely between the orbits of Jupiter and Saturn, giving it the path of a planet.

Left: Great Comet of 1843

COMETS appear 5 to 10 times each year. Most are telescopic objects, although the chances of seeing at least one large, bright comet during your life are good. Comets are the most primitive members of the solar system, containing material from its formation. They orbit the sun with periods ranging from a few years to tens of thousands of years.

The head of a comet is usually only a few miles across, and composed of a mixture of ices, rocks, and dust, surrounded by a gaseous cloud, the coma. When a comet nears the sun the heat boils off the ices and releases gases and dust. Pressure from sunlight and the solar wind cause these to stream away from the sun in the comet's tail, which always points away from the sun. Although hundreds of millions of miles long, the tail is very vaporous, and stars may be seen shining through it.

There are many short-period comets whose elliptical orbits lie within the orbits of the planets; all are faint. Astronomers think most comets originate in a huge cloud of billions of comets lying thousands of times farther from the sun than the earth. Occasionally a nearby star will disturb one and it will plunge into the inner solar system where we will see it. On each close approach to the sun a comet loses material, and some even split into two or more parts.

Some comets, called "sun-grazers," come closer to the sun than Mercury. Sometimes the massive Jupiter will change the orbit of the comet, capturing it within the inner solar system. Following comets in their orbits are often swarms of meteoroids; several meteor showers (p. 132) occur when the earth crosses cometary orbits.

Orbit of Jupiter

Sun

Path of Encke's Comet

METEORS are the flashes of light in the sky caused by the fiery plunge of particles of space debris into our atmosphere. In space such particles are termed meteoroids. As they hit the atmosphere a hundred miles up at a speed of 25 miles per second, they burn up.

About 5-10 sporadic meteors can be seen each hour on a dark night in a good location. Several times a year the earth passes through meteoroid swarms (usually along the orbits of comets) and we may see many more meteors per hour: a meteor shower (p. 132).

About 100 million meteoroids, a total of about 10 tons, hit earth each day. Most are the size of a grain of sand; brighter meteors may be about the size of a pea. Most meteoroids burn up, but a few are large enough to reach the ground as meteorites.

Large Iron Meteorite from Greenland: 34 Tons

Etched Surface of an Iron Meteorite

Meteor Crater, Arizona

METEORITES are meteoroids which have not completely burned up and have reached the earth. They range from microscopic dust to specimens weighing tons. Some are made of iron-nickel alloy (called irons); some are stony; a few rare ones are iron and stone (called stony-irons). The largest iron types are the Hoba meteorite in southwest Africa and the Anhighito meteorite, 34 tons, found in Greenland. The largest stony meteorites are much smaller. More stony meteorites fall than iron ones, but more iron ones are found, because they are more easily identified and resist weathering.

Earth is pockmarked with huge craters from ancient falls. In Arizona a crater 4,660 feet across and 626 feet deep was created by the fall of a 50,000 ton iron meteoroid. Even larger craters are known at Hudson Bay, in Europe, and elsewhere.

OBSERVING METEORS takes little equipment. They may be seen any clear night, though they are more frequent during showers. More are seen after midnight, because you are then on the leading side of the earth as it moves in its orbit. Occasionally there are extremely bright meteors, called bolides or fireballs, which light up the sky or can be seen in daytime. They often leave a smoke trail and sometimes produce a sound.

When observing, use comfortable lounge chairs, and dress warmly, even in summer. If you want to chart a shower it helps to have an observer and an assistant to record sightings. For each meteor, note its path, speed, duration, brightness compared to stars, starting and stopping point in the sky, color, whether it left a trail and how long it persisted.

IMPORTANT ANNUAL METEOR SHOWERS

Date	Shower		Location of radiant
Jan. 2-3	Quadrantids	E	Between Boötes and head of Draco
Apr. 20-22	Lyrids	NE	Between Vega and Hercules
May 4-6	Aquarids	E	SW of the Square of Pegasus
Aug. 10-13	Perseids	NE	Perseus
Oct. 8-10	Draconids	E	Brilliant in 1946. Period about 6½ years
Oct. 18-23	Orionids	E	Between Orion and Gemini
Nov. 8-10	Taurids	NE	Between Taurus, Auriga, and Perseus
Dec. 10-12	Geminids	E	Near Castor in Gemini

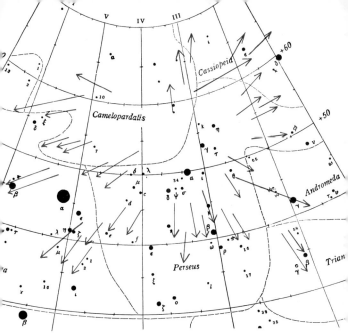

Perseid Shower Noted on American Meteor Society Chart

METEOR CHART   This is a chart of the paths that meteors seem to follow during a shower. Actually, the meteors move in parallel paths. These paths seem to emerge from a point — an optical illusion due to perspective. Meteors in a shower do originate in the same part of the sky, though they are not related to the constellation from which they seem to come. If the radiant point and the speed of the meteors are known, the orbit of the meteor swarm can be calculated. The more observations, the more accurately this can be done. Possibly most meteors belong to swarms and very few solitary, stray meteors exist.

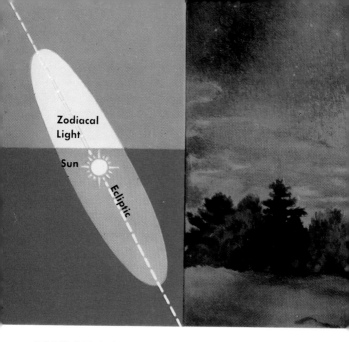

ZODIACAL LIGHT is so called because the triangular band of light which extends from the horizon halfway to the zenith follows the earth's ecliptic and hence passes through the constellations of the Zodiac. This very faint glowing light is best observed in the early evenings of March and April and just before dawn in September and October. In the tropics it is seen more often. On a clear, moonless night its brightest areas may outshine the Milky Way. In the above illustrations its brightness has been emphasized to show its form.

Zodiacal light is apparently sunlight reflected from meteoric particles existing in areas near the plane of the ecliptic. Though meteoric particles are concentrated in this

134

region, they are widely separated. If the particles were of pinhead size and five miles apart, there would be enough within the earth's orbit to reflect the amount of light usually observed.

The zodiacal light seems to widen into a spot some 10 degrees in diameter at a place just opposite the sun. This faint haze of light that moves opposite the sun is known as Gegenschein or Counterglow.

The area of zodiacal light called Gegenschein may owe its increased light to the fact that meteoric particles directly opposite the sun reflect toward us more sunlight than is reflected by particles in portions of the band that are not directly opposite the sun.

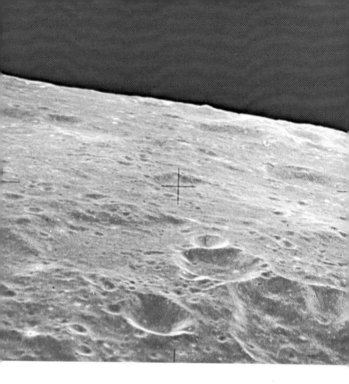

ON THE MOON   Our unique moon is over a quarter of the diameter of the planet around which it revolves. However, its weight is only 1/81 that of the earth, its volume 1/50, and its gravitional pull 1/6 of the earth's. No life forms have been found there. On the sunny side, temperatures are near boiling; on the dark side they are lower than any on earth. In some sections cindery, dusty plains extend in all directions, their surface marred by deep cracks and broken ridges. Thousands of craters, some caused by meteors, some perhaps by ancient volcanoes,

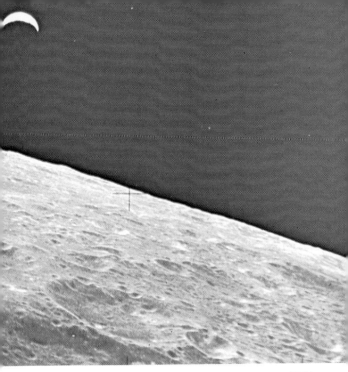

Earth Rising Over Lunar Horizon   NASA

cover the rest of the moon's surface. These range from ¼ mile to 150 miles across, with steep, rocky walls jutting upward as high as a mile or two. Sometimes an isolated peak is within the crater. Bright streaks or rays extend in all directions from some craters.

Besides the craters and plains (called seas by early astronomers who thought they were full of water), the moon has mountain ranges with peaks three, four, and five miles high. In proportion to the size of the moon, they are much higher than mountains on the earth.

BEYOND THE MOON lies the solar system. Much of it we have now explored with robot spacecraft, and we have studied stars and galaxies from orbiting observatories. But the moon remains the only other celestial object humans have explored in person.

U.S. and Soviet probes have descended through the hellish Venusian atmosphere and landed on its surface, some of the latter sending back color photographs.

Two U.S. Viking craft landed on Mars. They dug trenches, photographed its surface, and analyzed the soil and the atmosphere for signs of life, sending back years of meteorological data.

Two U.S. — launched Pioneer spacecraft, followed by two Voyager probes, flew through the asteroid belt, then whizzed around Jupiter. They obtained beautiful close photographs of the clouds and the satellites, discovering that Jupiter has a faint ring, and that one of its satellites, Io, is the most volcanic object we know of. These probes flew on to Saturn, and one continued on to Uranus. Around both planets the probes found more moons and complex ring systems than we had known. One of the Pioneer probes, still sending back data, is now outside the planetary system, the first man-made object to travel to the stars. One of the Voyager craft is now headed for rendezvous with Neptune.

Earth's atmosphere keeps certain types or radiation from reaching the surface. Orbiting telescopes, such as the Orbiting Solar Observatory, Gamma Ray Observatory, Uhuru ultraviolet observatory, and studies done aboard manned spacecraft have given us new views of the universe impossible to obtain in any other way. Space Telescope, in the late 1980s, will further greatly expand our horizons.

Left: Space Telescope Probes the Cosmos   NASA

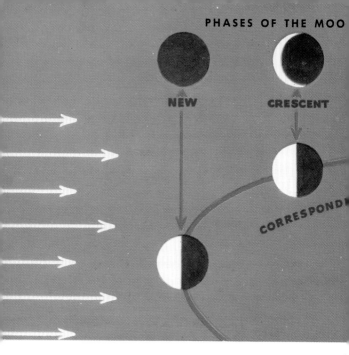

PHASES OF THE MOON   On the earth we see the moon change from crescent to full and back again in 29½ days. This is the origin of our word "month." If you were out in space, you would see that about half the moon is always lit up by the sun and half is always in darkness, except during an eclipse. When the moon is most directly between us and the sun, we see only the dark side. But, because the moon is revolving around the earth every 27⅓ days, varying amounts of the lighter side are seen.

When the earth is in line between the sun and the moon, we see the moon's fully illuminated side and can watch it as a full moon from sunset to the next sunrise. All other stages

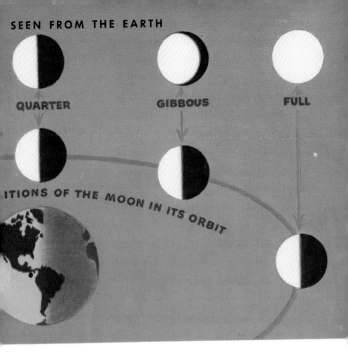

QUARTER

GIBBOUS

FULL

ITIONS OF THE MOON IN ITS ORBIT

are in between. When the moon is a quarter of the way around its orbit, we still see half its surface, but half of this half is dark and half is illuminated, giving us a quarter moon. When the moon is more than a quarter, but less than full, it is called "gibbous."

As the moon revolves around the earth, it rotates on its axis, keeping almost the same face turned toward us. A slight wobble of the moon, due mainly to a small difference between the times of revolution and rotation and to a tilt of the moon's axis, has allowed us to see from the earth a total of 59 percent of the moon's surface. Lunar probes have now mapped the entire surface.

141

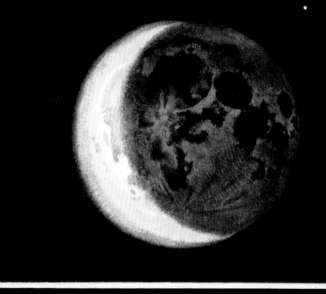

EARTHSHINE is light which has traveled from the sun to the earth, hence to the moon, and back again to the earth. Earthshine is very faint because only a small part of the sunlight reflected from the earth hits the moon. The moon reflects only 7 percent of this into space again and only a tiny fraction of this 7 percent finally comes back to earth. When you look for earthshine, note that the crescent moon, because it is brighter, seems larger.

142

LUNAR HALO   Rings around the sun and moon are often seen. These are in our atmosphere and are of the same general nature as rainbows. Halos are due to the refraction of sunlight or moonlight by thin, high, icy clouds. The halo making a 22-degree circle around the moon is the most common. A 46-degree circle may also form and, if the ice crystals in the clouds are just right, one may see arcs and other curious effects. Halos are usually colorless, but sometimes they appear like faint rainbows with the red on the inside.

TIDES   Every object in the universe exerts a gravitational pull on every other object. The force is greater the greater the masses of the objects, and decreases rapidly with distance. The two bodies with the greatest influence on the earth are the moon and sun. Their pulls cause the tides.

The pull of the moon is greater on the side of the earth facing the moon than it is on the center of the earth; the pull is also greater on the center of the earth than it is on a point on earth opposite the moon. This difference in pulls causes the tides. Roughly speaking, water on the side of earth nearest the moon is pulled away from the earth, while the earth itself is pulled away from water on the side away from the moon. This causes two tidal bulges of water on earth. The sun has a similar effect, but, because it is much farther away, the effect is less.

If the pulls of the sun and moon are aligned, near the times of new moon and full moon, the tidal bulge is higher, called "spring tide." If the sun and moon pull at right angles to each other, near the quarter moons, the tidal bulge is lower, called "neap tide."

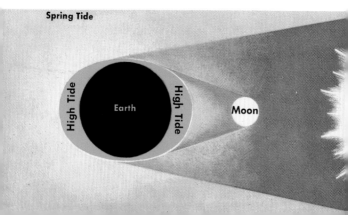

Earth

Moon

Neap Tide

Tides are also higher than usual at times of the month when the moon, in its elliptical orbit, is nearest earth.

The earth rotates underneath these tidal bulges, giving each coastal location on earth high and low tides each day. The exact timing and height of tides at any location depend also on the shape of the ocean basin and seacoast. Usually the tidal range (low tide to high tide) is 3 to 10 feet. In V-shaped bays, such as the Bay of Fundy, tides may rise 50 feet; in broad bays tides may rise and fall less than a foot.

Photograph of Moon Taken Through the 36-inch Refracting Telescope at the Lick Observatory. South is at the top.

Piccolor

MARE NECTARIS

Vendelinus
Langrenus

Theophilu

PYRENEES MTS.

MARE FOECUNDITATIS

MARE TRANQUILLITA

MARE CRISIUM

Posidoniu

LACUS SOMNIOR

EXPLORING THE MOON

The accompanying chart shows the moon as it might be seen through a low-power telescope. The majority of the various features mapped at this magnification can be seen also with a pair of good, high-power field glasses. Most craters and mountains on the moon have the names (often Latinized) of famous astronomers and other scientists. The dry "seas" have fanciful Latin names. Though the chart shows the full moon, studying it as suggested on p. 148 is most satisfactory.

KEY: Mountains, seas, and lakes are in SMALL CAPITALS
Craters and other features are in regular type

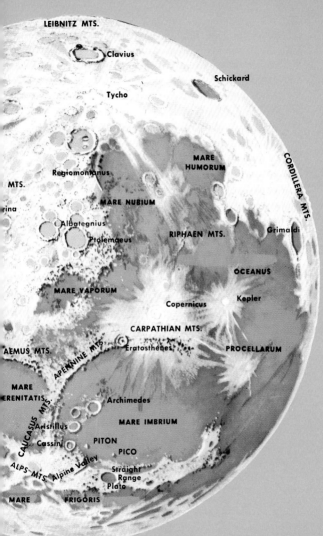

LEIBNITZ MTS.

Clavius

Schickard

Tycho

MARE HUMORUM

Regiomontanus

CORDILLERA MTS.

MTS.

MARE NUBIUM

rina

Albategnius

RIPHAEN MTS.

Grimaldi

Ptolemaeus

OCEANUS

MARE VAPORUM

Copernicus   Kepler

CARPATHIAN MTS.

AEMUS MTS.

APENNINE MTS.   Eratosthenes   PROCELLARUM

MARE
SERENITATIS

Archimedes

CAUCASUS MTS.

Aristillus   MARE IMBRIUM

Cassini   PITON

PICO

ALPS-MTS. Alpine Valley

Straight
Range
Plato

MARE   FRIGORIS

147

OBSERVING THE MOON With the photograph and map on pages 146-147 as a guide, you can easily study the moon and identify a dozen or two of the most prominent features. Even a pair of small field glasses will show the "seas," mountain ranges, and ringed plains, and the great craters. Larger field glasses or a small telescope will disclose all the features identified on the map.

The very best time to observe is in the two- or three-day period after the first quarter. The moon is then in a good position for evening study; nearly all major features can be seen and the moon is not sufficiently bright to cause loss of detail through glare. It is even better to follow the moon evening after evening from its first thin crescent until it is full. As the line of darkness recedes, features near the border stand out in bold relief; the shadows become stronger and details are more easily seen.

Should you pass this stage and desire to explore the moon further, more detailed maps are available. These divide the full moon up into sections and show you the features of each section. Over 500 features on the moon have been named. Its whole surface has been mapped. Detailed study will call your attention to interesting problems: the distribution of craters; the overlapping of some craters; the nature of rays on the moon; and the origin of the seas. Even though the moon is our nearest neighbor, there is much we have yet to learn about it. However, since we have visited the moon and brought back rocks from it, the newer explorations will probably be chemical rather than astronomical.

Label in image: Corona

Total Eclipse of the Sun Showing Prominences and Outer Corona

ECLIPSE OF THE SUN   Until recently no astronomical event offered such opportunities as a total eclipse of the sun. Using new methods, astronomers can now make some of the observations that once had to await an eclipse. But the beauty and awesomeness of a total eclipse are still un-equaled. In the pattern of movements of moon, earth, and sun, there are always two to five solar eclipses each year. Some are total, some partial, and some annular (p. 152). On the average there are two total eclipses of the sun every three years.

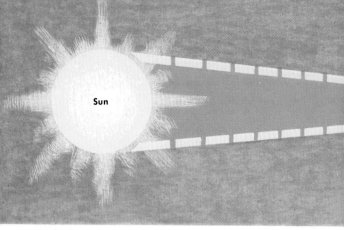

Total Eclipse of Sun

SOLAR ECLIPSE An eclipse of the sun can occur only when the moon is new — when it is between the earth and the sun. If the orbits of earth and moon were on exactly the same plane and if these two bodies were at their minimum distance apart, an eclipse would occur every month. It does not occur that often because the moon's orbit is inclined about 5 degrees to the earth's orbit. In addition, the moon's path takes it slightly nearer or farther from earth as it revolves. This is important, as the average length of the moon's shadow is 232,000 miles, but its distance from earth averages 235,000 miles. A total eclipse cannot occur under average conditions.

However, because of variations in its orbit, the moon's shadow is sometimes longer and its distance from earth sometimes shorter. If this occurs at the time of a new moon, we may have an eclipse. The time and place of earth eclipses are calculated years in advance. At any one place the duration of totality varies. The maximum possible

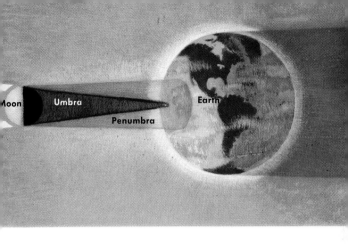

length of totality is about 7½ minutes. The path of a total eclipse will cross a given location roughly once every 350 years.

You will see a total eclipse when the true shadow (umbra) of the moon passes over you. The umbra produces a round shadow, never more than 170 miles in diameter, which travels rapidly over the earth. The penumbra, which surrounds the umbra like an inverted cone, does not completely exclude the sunlight and hence gives only a partial eclipse. It forms a circle about 4,000 miles in diameter around the umbra. Observers in the path of totality see a partial eclipse as the disc of the moon covers more and more of the sun's face. Then, at the moment of totality, red prominences appear. The weirdly darkened sky is lit up by the streaming corona, which may extend over a million miles from the sun's surface. Nothing is as inspiring and awesome as the few minutes of totality. Then, after repeating the partial phase, the eclipse is over.

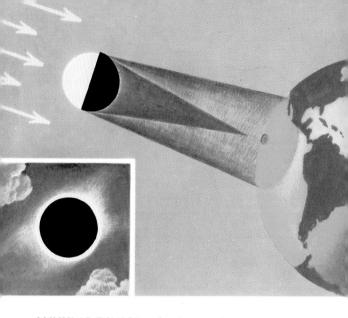

ANNULAR ECLIPSE The distance from the earth to the moon varies. If an eclipse occurs when the moon is its average distance away or farther, the umbra of the moon's shadow does not reach the earth. An annulus, or thin ring of sunlight, remains around the moon. The path of an annular eclipse is about 30 miles wider than that of a total eclipse. Surrounding this area, as in a total eclipse, is a region 4,000 to 6,000 miles wide where the eclipse is partial. Of all solar eclipses, about 35 percent are partial; 32 percent annular; 5 percent both annular and total; and 28 percent total.

Right: Paths for Total Solar Eclipses Through the End of the Century, and for the Next One Across the U.S.

Left: Annular Eclipse. Red Spot Shows Area in Which Annular Eclipse Is Seen; Elsewhere in the Penumbra Eclipse Is Partial

TOTAL ECLIPSES OF SUN

The movements of sun, moon, and earth causing eclipses are well known. They occur in a cycle of just over 18 years, after which a new series of eclipses repeats with only minor changes. One change is a westward shift with each new cycle. A knowledge of these cycles enables astronomers to predict eclipses hundreds of years in advance. Ancient eclipses are the most certain and useful of chronological data.

Partial solar eclipses visible in parts of North America occur on May 19, 1985, and March 7, 1989. No total eclipses occur over the continental U.S. until 2017; a very long total eclipse (6½ minutes) passes near Hawaii and across Mexico on July 11, 1991. Generally, you have to travel to see a total solar eclipse. Commercial tours are often available.

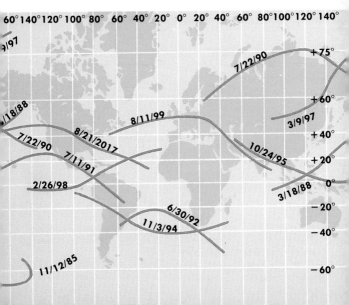

Total Eclipse of the Moon

LUNAR ECLIPSE The earth's shadow is some 900,000 miles long. When the moon enters into it and is eclipsed, the eclipse lasts as long as several hours and may be total for as much as 1 hour and 40 minutes. In any year there may be no eclipses of the moon or as many as two and rarely three. Though there are fewer eclipses of the moon than of the sun, they last longer and can be seen by more people over a wider area. Because some of the sunlight striking the earth is diffused and scattered by our atmosphere, the earth's shadow is not completely dark. Enough of this light reaches the moon to give it a faint coppery glow even when it is totally eclipsed. An eclipse of the moon occurs only at the time of full moon. Because of angles of the moon's orbit, it may miss the shadow

TOTAL LUNAR ECLIPSES

Date	Time of midpoint of eclipse (EST)	Duration of eclipse	Duration of totality
May 4, 1985	2:57 p.m.	3 h. 18 m.	68 m.
Oct. 28, 1985	12:43 p.m.	3 h. 34 m.	44 m.
Apr. 24, 1986	7:44 a.m.	3 h. 18 m.	64 m.
Oct. 17, 1986	2:19 p.m.	3 h. 36 m.	72 m.
Feb. 20, 1989	10:37 a.m.	3 h. 42 m.	78 m.
Aug. 16, 1989	10:09 p.m.	3 h. 34 m.	96 m.
Feb. 9, 1990	2:13 p.m.	3 h. 24 m.	42 m.

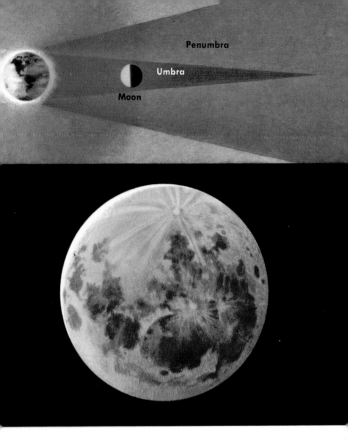

of the earth completely at that time, or it may only pass through the penumbra. A lunar eclipse offers proof of the earth's shape, for the umbra that passes over the moon has the distinct curve of a shadow of a ball.

The table shows total lunar eclipses for the rest of the decade.

THE CONSTELLATIONS

The 88 officially recognized constellations are listed below. All but a few appear on the star charts in this guide. Keep in mind that latitude, season, elevation, atmospheric conditions, and time of night all determine whether a constellation is visible.

If a constellation is too far south to be seen from most parts of the Northern Hemisphere, a figure is given which is the northern-most latitude at which the constellation (or most of it) can be seen under good conditions. Thus Crux can be seen south of about 25°N. latitude.

The best season for seeing the constellation is indicated by the date on which the constellation reaches its highest point above the horizon (the meridian) at 9 p.m. Each evening a constellation reaches the meridian about 4 minutes earlier. Thus Andromeda is on the meridian at 9 p.m. on Nov. 10; at about 8:56 p.m. on Nov. 11; at about 5 p.m. on Jan. 10.

Constellation	On Meridian 9 p.m.
Andromeda	Nov. 10
Antlia (The Pump) 50°N.	Apr. 5
Apus (The Bird of Paradise) 5°N.	June 30
Aquarius (The Water Bearer) 75°N.	Oct. 10
Aquila (The Eagle)	Aug. 30
Ara (The Altar) 30°N.	July 20
Aries (The Ram)	Dec. 10
Auriga (The Charioteer)	Jan. 30
Boötes (The Herdsman)	June 15
Caelum (The Burin) 45°N.	Jan. 15
Camelopardalis (The Giraffe)	Feb. 1
Cancer (The Crab)	Mar. 15
Canes Venatici (The Hunting Dogs)	May 20
Canis Major (The Big Dog) 65°N.	Feb. 15
Canis Minor (The Little Dog)	Mar. 1
Corona Borealis (Northern Crown)	June 30
Corvus (The Crow) 65°N.	May 10

Constellation	On Meridian 9 p.m.
Capricornus (The Goat, or the Sea Goat) 65°N.	Sept. 20
Carina (The Keel of the ship Argo, which is no longer a constellation) 25°N.	Mar. 15
Cassiopeia (The Queen)	Nov. 20
Centaurus (The Centaur) 35°N.	May 20
Cepheus (The King)	Oct. 15
Cetus (The Whale, or Sea Monster)	Nov. 30
Chamaeleon 5°N.	Apr. 15
Circinus (The Compasses) 25°N.	June 15
Columba (The Dove) 50°N.	Jan. 30
Coma Berenices (Berenice's Hair)	May 15
Corona Australis (Southern Crown) 45°N.	Aug. 15
Pegasus (The Winged Horse)	Oct. 20
Perseus	Dec. 25

Constellation	On Meridian 9 p.m.	Constellation	On Meridian 9 p.m.
Crater (The Cup) 70°N.	Apr. 25	Phoenix (The Phoenix) 40°N.	Nov. 20
Crux (The Cross) 25°N.	May 10	Pictor (The Easel) 30°N.	Jan. 20
Cygnus (The Swan)	Sept. 10	Pisces (The Fishes)	Nov. 10
Delphinus (The Dolphin)	Sept. 15	Pisces Austrinus (The Southern Fish) 55°N.	Oct. 10
Dorado (The Goldfish) 25°N.	Jan. 20	Puppis (The Stern of the ship Argo)	Feb. 25
Draco (The Dragon)	July 20	Pyxis (The Compass) 55°N.	Mar. 15
Equuleus (The Colt)	Sept. 20	Reticulum (The Net) 25°N.	Dec. 30
Eridanus (The River) 70°N.	Jan. 5	Sagitta (The Arrow)	Aug. 30
Fornax (The Furnace) 55°N.	Dec. 15	Sagittarius (The Archer) 60°N.	Aug. 20
Gemini (The Twins)	Feb. 20	Scorpius (The Scorpion) 55°N.	July 20
Grus (The Crane) 35°N.	Oct. 10	Sculptor 55°N.	Nov. 10
Hercules	July 25	Scutum (The Shield) 75°N.	Aug. 15
Horologium (The Clock) 25°N.	Dec. 25	Serpens (The Serpent) 85°N.	
Hydra (The Water Serpent) 70°N.	Apr. 20	Caput (Head)	June 30
Hydrus 15°N.	Dec. 10	Cauda (Tail)	Aug. 5
Indus (The Indian) 35°N.	Sept. 25	Sextans (The Sextant) 85°N.	Apr. 5
Lacerta (The Lizard)	Oct. 10	Taurus (The Bull)	Jan. 15
Leo (The Lion)	Apr. 10	Telescopium (The Telescope) 35°N.	Aug. 25
Leo Minor (The Little Lion)	Apr. 10	Triangulum (The Triangle)	Dec. 5
Lepus (The Hare) 65°N.	Jan. 25	Triangulum Australe (The Southern Triangle) 20°N.	July 5
Libra (The Scales) 70°N.	June 20	Tucana (The Toucan) 20°N.	Nov. 5
Lupus (The Wolf) 45°N.	June 20	Ursa Major (The Great Bear)	Apr. 20
Lynx (The Lynx)	Mar. 5	Ursa Minor (The Little Bear)	June 25
Lyra (The Lyre)	Aug. 15	Vela (The Sails of the ship Argo) 35°N.	Mar. 5
Mensa (The Table Mountain) 5°N.	Jan. 30	Virgo (The Virgin) 80°N.	May 25
Microscopium (The Microscope) 50°N.	Sept. 20	Volan (The Flying Fish) 15°N.	Mar. 1
Monoceros (The Unicorn) 85°N.	Feb. 20	Vulpecula (The Fox)	Sept. 10
Musca (The Fly) 15°N.	May 10		
Norma (The Level) 35°N.	July 5		
Octans (The Octant) 5°N.	Sept. 20		
Ophiuchus (The Serpent Bearer) 85°N.	July 25		
Orion (The Hunter) 85°N.	Jan. 25		
Pavo (The Peacock) 20°N.	Aug. 25		

OBJECTS FOR OBSERVATION

VISIBLE THROUGH THE YEAR (Middle North Latitudes)

Constellations: See seasonal charts, pp. 54-99. Learn first those with brighter stars.
Bright Stars: See list, p. 35, and seasonal charts. Identify star types by color (p.37). Estimate magnitudes by comparison.
The Moon: Detailed suggestions on p. 148. Map, pp. 146-147.
Milky Way: Binoculars resolve much of milkiness into thousands of stars. Note dark nebulae between Cygnus and Scorpius, and star fields in Cygnus and Sagittarius.

Asteroids: Positions given in astronomical periodicals. Large asteroids, when near earth, can be spotted with binoculars.
Planets: See pp. 124-125. Use binoculars for 4 of Jupiter's moons and Venus' crescent; telescope for Saturn's rings. Positions of Uranus and Neptune given in astronomical periodicals.
Meteors: Table of showers, p. 132. Suggestions, pp. 132-133.
Mizar: (star): In Big Dipper, p. 64. Note companion, Alcor.

VISIBLE DURING PART OF THE YEAR (Middle North Latitudes)

The celestial objects listed below are at the meridian at 9 p.m. standard time during the months indicated. They are visible in middle latitudes for one or more months before and after the months indicated. Their positions when observed depend on your latitude and the hour of observation.

January
Pleiades (open cluster): Near Perseus, pp. 82 and 86.
Hyades (open cluster): In Taurus, pp. 90-91, 93. Easy for naked eye.
M42 (Great Nebula): In Orion, pp. 90, 92. Impressive in binoculars.
Betelgeuse (variable red giant): In Orion, pp. 90, 92. Compare with Rigel (mag. 0.3, p. 92) and Procyon (mag. 0.5, p. 95).

February
M35 (open cluster): In Gemini, near Castor's left foot, pp. 65, 66.

March
M44 (open cluster): In Cancer, in center of "square," p. 64. Called Praesepe or Beehive. Splendid in binoculars.

May
Coma Berenices (open cluster): Between Leo and Boötes, pp. 64-65. Use binoculars.

July
M13 (globular cluster): In Hercules, pp. 72, 74. Faint, fuzzy spot.

Binoculars show glowing cloud; telescope, individual stars.
M6 and M7 (open clusters): In Scorpius (pp. 72, 76), 5° northeast of tip of tail. Fine in binoculars.

August
Epsilon Lyrae (double star): In Lyra, 2° northeast of Vega, pp. 72, 75. Close pair. Telescope shows each is a double.

September
Albireo (double star): In Cygnus, p. 78. Small telescope reveals pair, orange and blue. Superb.

November
M31 (Great Spiral Nebula in Andromeda): See p. 85. Small, faint spot to unaided eye; glowing cloud in binoculars.

December
Double cluster in Perseus: In center of Perseus, p. 82. Faint, hazy patch becomes, in binoculars, a splendid spray of stars.
Algol (eclipsing variable): In Perseus, p. 86. Observe magnitude changes. Compare with Polaris (mag. 2.1).

INDEX

Bold type denotes pages containing more extensive information.

160